# Hiking
# Virginia

*by*
**Randy Johnson**

(Formerly *The Hiker's Guide to Virginia*)

FALCON™

Falcon Press® Publishing Co., Inc.,
Helena, Montana

# A FALCON GUIDE

Falcon Press is continually expanding its list of recreational guidebooks. All books include detailed descriptions, accurate maps, and all the information neccessary for enjoyable trips. You can order extra copies of this book and get information and prices for other Falcon guidebooks by writing Falcon Press, P.O. Box 1718, Helena, MT 59624 or calling toll-free 1-800-582-2665. Also, please ask for a free copy of our current catalog.

All photos and maps by author unless otherwise noted.
Cover photo: The Blue Ridge and the Great Valley of Virginia from
Buzzards Roost, Sharp Top Trail, by Randy Johnson

ISBN 1-56044-435-5

 Text pages printed on recycled paper

## CAUTION

Outdoor recreation activities are by their very nature potentially hazardous. All participants in such activities must assume the responsibility for their own actions and safety. The information contained in this guidebook cannot replace sound judgment and good decision– making skills, which help reduce risk exposure, nor does the scope of this book allow for disclosure of all the potential hazards and risks involved in such activities.

Learn as much as possible about the outdoor recreation activities you participate in, prepare for the unexpected, and be safe and cautious. The reward will be a safer and more enjoyable experience.

# CONTENTS

**Editor's note:** Because Falcon Press reprints its guidebooks regularly with updates of trail data, addresses, and phone numbers, we encourage interested readers to report any recent trail changes or comments. Please contact the publisher and the author at the address listed on the copyright page. The author can be reached via e-mail at: ranjohns@aol.com

# LOCATOR MAP

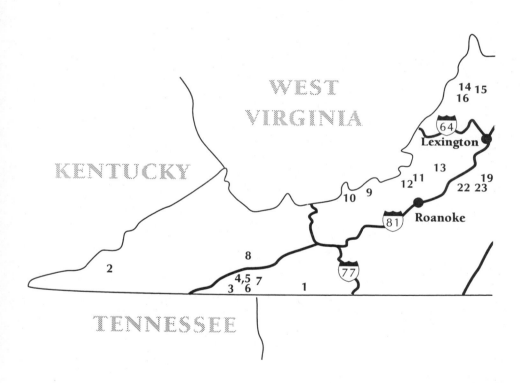

Winchester

Washington, D. C.

66   46

81

45
42
43
44

28
30, 31
27   29

17,18

26

29

95

47

52

25
21 24

Charlottesville

35 34
33

20
32

29

64

Richmond
41

13

36

39
40

Lynchburg   37   Petersburg
38

48   49
50
51

Norfolk

85

ATLANTIC
OCEAN

NORTH CAROLINA

*To my son Christopher—*

*May your trail find the summit free of
clouds, and views of new horizons.*

# INTRODUCTION

From the snow-drifted summit of Virginia's highest peak, to lighthouse-lit sand spits on the Atlantic, the Old Dominion can still be experienced much as it was when Native Americans trod the forests and new settlers marveled at virgin wilderness.

The early settlers, the first to "permanently" colonize the New World, strode away from beaches and riverbanks into what to them was a forbidding landscape, but all of that has changed. Today, urbanites flee to what little wild land remains, in search of scenic simplicity, if not literal solitude.

Luckily, Virginia's mountains, coast, and the regions in between have trails and deep woodlands reclaimed from earlier development. The vast virgin forests are gone, but tiny treasured islands of towering, uncut timber still remain. Hikers can stand beneath virgin hemlocks that were living when George Washington surveyed nearby forests for Lord Fairfax.

This book guides you to and on the best of these paths. Your options range from the mountains to the sea. There are short walks that focus on history or nature, and longer hikes that reach landmarks of national significance. The time needed to enjoy these walks ranges from a few minutes, for a nature trail, to a number of days for a rugged backpacking trip. Whichever type of hike you choose, Virginia's diverse scenery will captivate you.

Hiking in the mountains is the first option to tempt many hikers. Mountain forests, even those clearcut in the early part of the century, have grown back to pristine beauty under the stewardship of the National Park Service and USDA Forest Service. The most prominent areas managed by those agencies include the George Washington and Jefferson national forests (both of which include federally designated wilderness areas), Shenandoah National Park, and the Blue Ridge Parkway.

Heading west from the urban corridor that runs from Washington, DC, through Richmond to Norfolk, the first range of mountains is the distinctive, largely single spine of the Blue Ridge. The highest of these peaks is in the neighborhood of 4,000 feet, and the Blue Ridge Parkway and Skyline Drive meander along that crest.

Beyond this "front range" of the Appalachians lies a tremendous valley called the Shenandoah Valley in the north and the Great Valley in the south.

Beyond the valley, the Alleghenies rise to meet the border with West Virginia. The greatest jumble of these peaks scatters across the mountainous coal country of the state's southwestern triangle. Virginia's highest summit, Mount Rogers (5,729 feet), abuts the North Carolina border.

Some of Eastern America's most noteworthy trails delve into these storied mountains. Scenery ranges from near-alpine vistas of crag-capped meadows to the more intimate, and stereotypical, forested summits of Appalachia. Secluded campsites, backpacking shelters, and even overnight cabins tempt backpackers.

Virginia's other federally owned lands include a national seashore, national historic sites and historical parks, national monuments, parkways, a forest park, and national wildlife refuges. More than half of the battles in the Civil War were fought in Virginia and federally owned battlefields, battlefield parks, and national military parks seem to be everywhere. Trails lead through now

*Many trails in Virginia national forests pass historic sites, like this old iron furnace in use before the Civil War.*

quiet forests once torn with gunfire. Many of these sites preserve woodland trails within sight of urban areas.

Virginia's exemplary state park system complements that federal land, and likewise spans the state. Virginia state parks have accessibly inexpensive facilities for outdoor vacations, including cabins and campgrounds. Trails are particularly well developed on state land. You'll find rocky paths across jagged peaks and boardwalk routes through seashore swamps. Some trails lead hikers on paths frequented by America's first settlers and Founding Fathers.

There is an extensive array of regional parks, too, and substantial private land is open to the hiker. Together, all of the parklands offer a statewide list of paths that place nearly every Virginian within a few minutes drive of an enjoyable hike.

Luckily, hiking is a year-round activity in Virginia's temperate mid-Atlantic climate. Winter frequently brings mild days to all parts of the state, especially the sandy Eastern Shore, Atlantic beaches, and the tide-influenced riverbank peninsulas called the Tidewater. Even cold February days in the mountains can bring nice hiking weather to the more easterly foothills and flatlands of the Piedmont.

However, elevations range up to nearly 6,000 feet in Virginia, and substantial snow falls on mountain summits, though inconsistently. On the highest peaks, there can be sunny February days when temperatures reach the fifties. Nevertheless, average annual snowfall on the summits of the Blue Ridge in the area of Shenandoah National Park is around forty inches, about the average accumulation in Chicago. Average annual snowfall is nearly eighty inches in the southwestern mountains, a yearly total reminiscent of snowfall totals in

Buffalo, New York. Storms can be accompanied by sub-zero cold.

In the Old Dominion's wildest places, that kind of climate can test the most serious winter backpacker or cross-country skier. Some of the trails mentioned in this book are suitable for cross-country skiing and that is mentioned. Though sporadic, stretches of cold and snowy weather are the norm, especially in January and February. The skier and winter hiker will want to focus on those months and be ready to go when the snow strikes. Winter hikers, especially those parking at high elevations or in remote areas, should be careful to equip their cars for winter conditions and park pointing downhill. The Blue Ridge Parkway and Skyline Drive can both be closed during inclement weather, with the central section of Shenandoah National Park having the greatest priority for snowplowing.

Hikers heading for the highest trails during the worst winter weather should be as capable and experienced at winter camping as hikers heading to New England. Severe cold and high winds, especially on alpine-like summits such as Mount Rogers, can quickly cause hypothermia and frostbite. Hikers have died from exposure in the Old Dominion.

Winter campers should take a pump-pressurized backpacking stove and not plan to rely on a campfire. Newly available clothing made of synthetic materials that stay warm even when wet, like polypropylene, are recommended for winter use.

Accumulating snowfall east of the mountains is an unusual event. The foothills and northern Piedmont receive some accumulation most winters, but it rarely stays more than a day. On the coast, snowcover is rare.

The spring months, especially March, can bring substantial snow to the highest peaks. As a rule, the mountains are well past winter by early April,

*Naturalist Doug Coleman leads a wildflower walk at Wintergreen Resort, a noteworthy private development in the Blue Ridge.*

though nights can be cold. April finds the state experiencing a spectacular explosion of spring blooms.

Summer can be brutally hot in the Piedmont and along the coast, with the hottest days reaching into the high nineties. The highest mountains escape that kind of heat and have a historic resort industry based on a cool summer climate. In fact, approach the highest mountains with ample clothing and rain gear, even in summer. Nights can dip into the fifties, and thunderstorms can cause cold rain and a high risk of electrocution, especially on exposed ridgetops. Elsewhere in the state, the danger of lightning is greatest in open areas.

Ticks are another summertime problem for hikers statewide. Walkers have the greatest likelihood of picking up the pests in the Piedmont and Tidewater. The danger of contracting diseases like Rocky Mountain spotted fever from ticks makes it worthwhile to stop and check for the pests, often when necessary. Other insects, including mosquitoes and even black flies at the highest peaks, can also be annoying in the spring and summer. Insect repellent can serve as an effective first line of defense against all the pests mentioned above.

Poisonous snakes can also be found across the state, with the copperhead being the most prevalent. The timber rattlesnake is seen in the mountains, but rarely, and the cottonmouth moccasin is a very poisonous viper found in swampy portions of the southeastern part of the state.

Autumn usually finds the snakes and insects on the wane with brilliant color capturing the hiker's attention. Color spreads from north to south, and west to east across the state. The best color occurs among the maples, birches, and beeches of the highest mountains, particularly in the southwest, near the border with North Carolina, and in the more northerly Alleghenies along the border with West Virginia.

Autumn is also when hikers should be most careful of forest fires. A dry, hot summer can make the problem particularly severe. Campfires are permitted throughout the state, except during burning bans most often instituted during autumn. Campfires are banned year round in certain parts of Shenandoah National Park and other areas deemed overused by backpackers.

In general, backpackers are encouraged to use gas backpacking stoves. They do away with the need to scavenge fuel in the woods, making them a more environmentally sound way to visit the natural areas described in this book. They also do away with an unsightly campfire ring, making the temporary wilderness campsite appear less visible, and therefore less likely to become permanent. Relatively few areas are actually closed to backpack camping, with the exceptions being Blue Ridge Parkway trails and certain mountaintops and backpacking shelters in Shenandoah National Park.

Only in Shenandoah National Park are hikers likely to see the state's native black bears. And only car campers at campgrounds in that park are likely to be pestered by bears looking for food. Rangers recommend taking the usual precaution of hanging your food from a limb away from the trunk of a tree using a length of rope.

Even casual hikers should keep certain precautions in mind. Only the easiest trails should be attempted in anything less than light hiking boots. Open sandals, even in warm weather, are generally not adequate for rocky trails or even areas where briars, ticks, or snakes might be encountered.

*This sign in Westmoreland State Park entices hikers to soak up the sounds of nature.*

Luckily, the trend is toward lightweight, sturdy hiking boots.

Hikers should carry a day pack with the usual items, such as food, a flashlight, rain gear, and a map. A canteen should be carried, and remember to avoid all but the most formalized water sources. Streams in even pristine areas can be affected by human pollution or animal waste. Definitely acquire any needed trail or camping permit before hiking. The trail descriptions include outstanding special regulations, but management policies change. Always check with forest or park managers before hiking, even if you just stop at the visitor center or ask a few questions at the entrance station.

*On the highest peaks in the state, hoar frost, or rime ice, often coats the trees in winter.*

After all of the essentials are packed, don't forget a camera or binoculars. Scenery aside, wildlife on Virginia's trails ranges from skunks, opossums, and raccoons to deer, bobcats, turkeys, and bears. Brands are diverse, but miniaturization is making once heavy cameras and binoculars a must for trail users. Of course, part of the joy of hiking is that you need very little in the way of official equipment, and for many of Virginia's easier trails, that is particularly true.

Where safety registration systems exist, check in, and especially out, with rangers or park personnel. Where no registration system is in place, consider leaving word with a responsible friend who can be counted on to contact authorities if you do not return by an agreed upon time. And by all means call ahead if you are going to return late. Hikers would be surprised how much time is wasted by rangers looking for hikers who aren't lost, but relaxing at home.

But wherever you roam, take with you a sense of exploration and appreciation. Many dedicated people, some of them citizen volunteers, have labored long to build trails or see that particular parks or forests have been preserved for hiking. Repay that effort with enjoyment and support it with a respectful obedience to the trail enthusiasts' dictum: take only pictures, leave only footprints. Once you've had the chance to fully explore the scenic beauty of the Old Dominion, you'll wonder how anyone could throw litter on trails and highways, or deface campsites and trail signs.

# MAP LEGEND

| | | | |
|---|---|---|---|
| Roads | | Shelter | □ |
| | | Building | ■ |
| Bridge | | Mine | ⊙ |
| Parking | P■ | Pass or Saddle | |
| Hiking Trail | | Mountain | ▲ |
| Appalachian Trail | | River, Creek, Drainage | |
| Bike Trail | | | |
| Horse Trail | | Lakes | |
| Trail Bridges | | Meadow | |
| Overlook | | Springs | |
| Campground | ▲ | Wilderness or Park Boundary | |

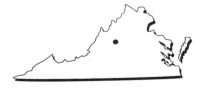

State of Virginia's outline
for approximate location of hike.

# VIRGINIA'S
# NATIONAL FORESTS

Virginia's two national forests total nearly 1.8 million acres, all of it in the western sweep of the state. Administratively, the two merged in 1995.

The 1.1-million-acre George Washington National Forest runs from the vicinity of Front Royal, in the north, to the James River in the south. The most easterly section lies on the Blue Ridge, providing a corridor for the Blue Ridge Parkway. In the west, lands of the George Washington National Forest skip over the mostly private land in the Shenandoah Valley and cover the Allegheny Mountains.

The eastern border of the George Washington National Forest reaches from just south of Shenandoah National Park to near Lynchburg. On the west, the "GW" follows the border with West Virginia much of the way from Winchester to Covington.

The 705,000 acres of the Jefferson National Forest cluster in four areas south of the George Washington. Smaller parcels perch on the Blue Ridge, northeast of Roanoke, and near the border with Kentucky, surrounding Norton.

The largest tract runs the West Virginia state line south, north of Interstate 81 and the Great Valley of Virginia. East of that, south of I-81, and bordering Tennessee, is the Mount Rogers National Recreation Area. This special area is given over almost exclusively to recreation, unlike other parts of both forests where timber harvesting is part of the mix of multiple uses.

The merged forest has six districts. Together, they boast very close to 2,000 miles of trails. The Jefferson claims, 1,035 miles, and the George Washington another 900 miles. There are fifteen federally designated wilderness areas in the forest. Their names run a tempting gamut of titles such as Mountain Lake, Rich Hole, Thunder Ridge, Beartown, James River Face, Rough Mountain, and Ramseys Draft.

A rough total of 81,000 acres of land is designated as wilderness in the national forest, a management category that prohibits motorized access and permanent manmade conveniences.

The original Wilderness Act of 1964 stipulated that the Wilderness designation be applied to pristine tracts largely untouched by man. Eastern Wilderness legislation in 1975 amended that to permit the protection of even previously logged areas. That permitted Virginia areas to qualify, but don't expect the Old Dominion's wilderness areas to be strictly re-grown woodlands. In fact, virgin timber and largely untouched forests are included in a number of the state's wildernesses.

Trails lace these wild lands, but many are only lightly maintained. Also, a number of wilderness areas have very few trails, or trail systems that just pass through or by the parcels. That, and the absence of good circuit hikes in some areas often accounts for their absence from this book.

For those truly in search of solitude and challenge, pathless wilderness areas offer a wealth of virtually unvisited ridgetops and stream valleys. Where Wilderness areas are covered in this book, some of those trailless hikes are mentioned. In the cases of Ramseys Draft and St. Mary's wilderness areas,

*The Appalachian Trail is a tempting and challenging landmark among Virginia's miles of trails.* L. Melancon/U.S.D.A. Forest Service photo.

the Forest Service offers glossy, full-colored wilderness topographical maps for sale.

Where wilderness areas are not mentioned, the forest supervisor or local ranger districts can supply free, photocopied pamphlets about the areas. These include a black-and-white topographical map.

Much to their credit, officials of Virginia's national forests work very closely with the Virginia Wilderness Committee, a citizen group of wilderness preservationists who have been instrumental since the mid-1970s in the preservation of the state's wild areas.

The group has a great deal of input into management as well, and has been active since the 1975 Eastern Wilderness legislation named James River Face as Virginia's first wilderness area. Since then, wilderness legislation has added new national forest areas in 1984 and again in 1988.

You needn't follow the lure of the name "Wilderness" to find good hiking in Virginia's national forests. Many wilderness trails are overly popular, and hikers can have just as fine an experience elsewhere in the forest. Both popular and little used trails are covered in this book, in and out of wilderness areas. Often suggestions are included for where, or when to hike to avoid crowds.

Together with National Forest trail managers, the citizen volunteers of the Wilderness Committee and other groups perform much of the trail maintenance required on national forest land. To help out in the National Forest trail effort, contact local ranger districts, the Virginia Wilderness Committee (write VWC, Rt. 1, Box 156, Swoope, VA 24479) and the Appalachian Trail Conference (see entry for Appalachian Trail).

Years of deficient funding have largely shifted trail maintenance on public land to private groups of concerned hikers. Though these volunteers struggle mightily, trails can be surprisingly overgrown, signs can be missing and storms can cause damage that goes unrepaired for some time. It wouldn't hurt to call the local ranger before hiking to check on the latest conditions.

The ranger districts can provide substantial detailed information. The headquarters for the forests, the supervisor's office, can provide a wide range of maps and general materials that introduce the developed facilities that hikers might use during a visit to the forest. Among these are many day use picnic areas that are not open to camping.

Most campgrounds, lakeshore recreation sites, facilities with running water restrooms, and the forest's few visitor centers ( Mount Rogers National Recreation Area/Massanutten Mountain/Glenwood District) are generally open and staffed from Memorial Day to Labor Day, with others open from May through October. Still others have what might appear to be unusual opening and closing dates geared to hunting seasons or other considerations. Some developed facilities are open year-round.

The latest hours of operation and current charges are available in written form with one phone call to the forest supervisor.

Large scale maps of the forests are also available, and they show the forest roads that explore the most remote, and often the most scenic areas of the forest. These numbered forest roads, or forest development roads, are abbreviated FDR in the book entries that describe individual hikes.

Generally, maps of all kinds are available in a price range between free and $3 or $5, depending on what you want. Individual districts offer most maps, as do the forest supervisor's office. Among the maps available is a $4 color

*Great hiking opportunities exist near metropolitan areas. Washington and Old Dominion Railroad Regional Park.*

map of the entire forest showing major forest roads, developed recreation sites, and points of interest. Charts describe recreation site facilities.

District Sportsmen's maps are currently available for about $4. These show rough elevations, recreation areas, highways, and major forest roads with emphasis on fishing and hunting. Big, glossy recreation maps, now $4, are large scale, show the full spectrum of forest roads, recreation sites, public highways, and have topographical detail. Appalachian Trail maps (see the entry for Appalachian Trail) showing portions of the trail are currently available for $6.

Special maps for the Ramseys Draft and St. Mary's Wilderness areas are available, $4 and $5 apiece, respectively. Individual topographical quadrangle maps, the best bet for trailless exploring, are also available from the forest service for many parts of the forest at $5. Many backpacking shops also carry these maps. Current prices, and details on availability, can be obtained from the following addresses and phone numbers.

Supervisor
George Washington and Jefferson
National Forests
Valleypointe Parkway
5162 Roanoke, VA 24019
(540) 857-2270

Deerfield Ranger District
Route 6, Box 419
Staunton, VA 24401
(540) 885-8028

Dry River Ranger District
112 N. River Road
Bridgewater, VA 22812
(540) 828-2591

James River Ranger District
810-A Madison Ave.
Covington, VA 24426
(540) 962-2214

Blacksburg Ranger District
110 Southpark Drive
Blacksburg, VA 24060-6648
(540) 552-4641

Clinch Ranger District
9416 Darden Dr.
Wise, VA 24293
(540) 328-2931

Glenwood Ranger District
P.O. Box 10
Natural Bridge Station, VA 24579
(540) 291-1806

Mount Rogers National Recreation
Area
Route 1, Box 303
Marion, VA 24354
(540) 783-5196

Lee Ranger District
109 Molineu Road
Edinburg, VA 22824
(540) 984-4101

Pedlar Ranger District
2424 Magnolia Avenue
Buena Vista, VA 24416
(540) 261-6105

Warm Springs Ranger District
Route 2, Box 30
Highway 220 South
Hot Springs, VA 24445
(540) 839-2521

Massanutten Visitor Center
3220 Lee Highway
New Market, VA 22844
(540) 740-8310 (May-Oct)

New Castle Ranger District
Box 246
New Castle, VA 24127
(540) 864-5195

Wythe Ranger District
155 Sherwood Forest Road
Wytheville, VA 24382
(540) 228-5551

Highlands Gateway Visitor
Center
Factory Merchants Mall
Drawer B-12
Max Meadows, VA 24360
(800) 446-9670

# THE HIKES

*The Virginia Creeper Trail from Abingdon to Mount Rogers, combines wilderness and easy walking.* Robert Neelands/U.S.D.A. Forest Service photo.

# HIKE 1    *STONE MOUNTAIN TRAIL, LAKE KEOKEE TRAIL; AND APPALACHIA LOOP*

**General description:** The Stone Mountain Trail is a spectacular eleven-mile end to end ridgetop hike with summit views at High Knob (2,900 feet) and virgin hemlocks along Roaring Branch. The trail connects to an easy four-mile loop hike around Lake Keokee, and both trails are near the moderate four-mile Appalachia Loop Trail.

**Elevation gain and loss:** Approximately 2,350 feet for Stone Mountain Trail.

**Trailhead elevation:** Approximately 1,850 feet at recommended starting point on U.S. 23/U.S. 58A. Approximately 1,600 feet at Cave Springs Recreation Area on State Route 621/FDR 107.

**High point:** Approximately 2,900 feet at High Knob on Big Stone Mountain Trail.

**Low point:** Approximately 2,600 feet at Olinger Gap and connection to Keokee Lake Trail.

**Water availability:** Trail follows stream from trailhead on U.S. 23/U.S. 58A, but water must be treated. Water is available in season at Cave Springs Recreation Area developed facilities, including a forty-two-site campground, small pond, swimming beach, and bathhouse. Water is available many places in the Appalachia/Big Stone Gap area.

**Finding the trailheads:** Recommended start for hike to Cave Springs Recreation Area is trailhead on U.S. 23/U.S. 58A between Appalachia and Big Stone Gap, at Roaring Branch. There is no parking here; use old dumpster/flea market parking spot nearby on the Big Stone Gap side of the trailhead.

To reach Cave Springs Recreation Area trailhead, go west of Big Stone Gap on U.S. 58A 2.5 miles to a right turn onto State Route 621. Cave Springs is 6.5 miles, with the last .5 mile on FDR 107 after a right turn.

**The hike:** This moderate to strenuous, eleven-mile day hike or overnight backpacking trip offers some of the best views in southwestern Virginia. The classic mountain towns of Appalachia and Big Stone Gap, and attractions such as the Southwest Virginia Museum Historical State Park, add cultural insight to scenic hiking.

The hike starts between Appalachia and Big Stone Gap near the latter town's namesake gap. The trail rises gradually up tumbling Roaring Branch through a more than 300-year-old hemlock forest. The trail climbs stone steps built by the YCC in the 1970's, and passes many small cascades.

The climb steepens and reaches High Knob, a spectacular crag, at about 2,900 feet, that boasts one of southwestern Virginia's best views. Hikers can see Big Stone Gap and the Powell River Gap to the south. To the northwest stands Black Mountain, Kentucky's highest peak at 4,145 feet. Views also reach to Bristol and the Great Valley of Virginia. Retracing your steps from here creates a nice easy to moderate day hike.

Beyond High Knob, the trail drops to Olinger Gap and a side trail goes northwest to Lake Keokee, the site of an easy four-mile loop trail around a ninety-two acre lake. The lake is known for superb fishing, with muskie, catfish, bass, and bluegill among the most plentiful species.

The lake shore parking area has vault toilets, picnic tables, and a trailhead. To reach this very easy path, take U.S. 23/U.S. 58A southwest from Appalachia about one mile to a right turn on VA 68. Take VA 68 for about seven miles, then continue on State Route 606 for two miles to State Route 623. Turn left on State Route 623 for about one mile to the lake.

Continuing on the Stone Mountain Trail beyond Olinger Gap, the hike follows an easy ridgeline. Between High Knob and Cave Springs Recreation Area, backpackers will notice a dozen good campsites.

Nearing Cave Springs, the trail drops off the ridge and meanders through a long series of switchbacks that reduce the grade. The trail reaches the eleven-mile mark, approximately 1,600 feet, at the Cave Springs Recreation Area, actually the site of an interesting cave. More energetic day hikers could start here, hike to High Knob and create a strenuous day hike.

## The Appalachia Loop Trail

This moderate four-mile loop trail climbs an old streamside road grade .2 mile to a junction with a rocky, sometimes steep loop hike that reaches a lookout from Little Stone Mountain. There are good views of surrounding

# HIKE 1 — STONE MOUNTAIN TRAIL, LAKE KEOKEE TRAIL, AND APPALACHIA LOOP HIKE

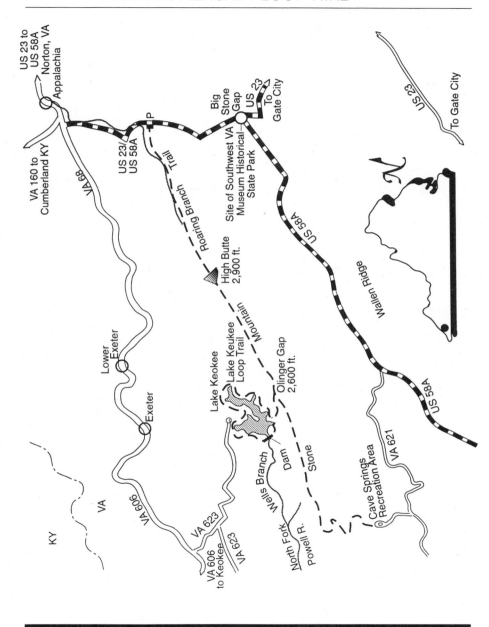

*Hikers should be prepared for winter storms when hiking in late fall in the mountains of southwest Virginia.*

mountains, and even Black Mountain in Kentucky. This summit is actually the neighboring peak to Stone Mountain, the hike described above, just across Big Stone Gap.

To reach the Appalachia Loop Trail, take U.S. 23/U.S. 58A southwest from Appalachia for about .5 mile to a left turn onto T-1321. At the end of the road, turn left onto T-1319 for one block, then right onto T-1322, Cold Springs Drive. Follow T-1322 to the end of the road and park on the side of the road near the trail.

# HIKE 2 *THE DEVILS FORK TRAIL SYSTEM*

**General description:** A moderate three-, four-, and six-mile hike that includes the Devils Bathtub, an unusual tub carved by water in solid rock. The hike also features a virgin hemlock forest of impressive size.

**Elevation gain and loss:** Approximately 1,400 feet.

**Trailhead elevation:** Approximately 1,800 feet.

**High point:** Approximately 2,500 feet.

**Water availability:** Water is available from streams along two-thirds of this hike, but it must be treated. Nearby Carter's Store and the town of Ka (pronounced KAY) are other water sources.

**Finding the trailhead:** From the north, the trail is located approximately eight miles south of Norton on State Route 619. From the south, the trailhead is about .7 mile north of Ka, the junction of State Route 619 and State Route 653.

## HIKE 2 *THE DEVILS FORK TRAIL SYSTEM*

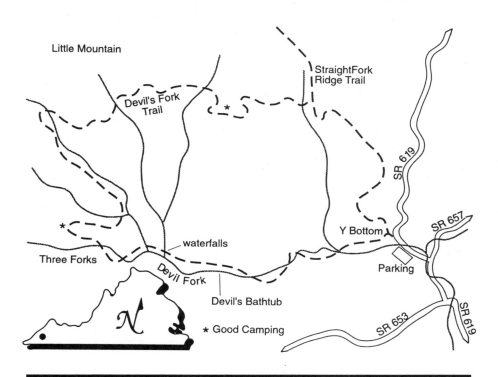

**The hike:** The Devils Fork Trail System is a four-mile loop hike along Devils Fork and a two-mile side trail to FDR 237 atop Little Mountain. The loop starts at a developed trailhead and splits at Y-Bottom, the confluence of Devils Fork and another stream where an old homesite is marked by an interpretive sign.

Taking the left side of the trail, the path is actually an old logging and coal mining railroad grade that threads its way up the tumbling stream past towering 300-year-old hemlock trees. Spectacular scenery, many stream crossings, and an easy grade distinguish this trail.

At 1.5 miles, hikers reach a long cascade that empties into the Devils Bathtub, a deep tub carved out of solid rock by swirling water. A return trip from here makes a nice, easy to moderate day hike.

Farther along, you reach the mouth of Corder Hollow and a twenty-foot waterfall. Beyond that, at Three Forks, three drainages meet, and hikers who look carefully may see the rotting timbers of an old railroad trestle. Others may notice a rusting coal car.

A good backpacking site is just beyond Three Forks, and then the trail swings away from the stream and slabs across the mountainside to its high point. Another fine campsite is located in this area.

The trail eventually reaches a junction on the left with the Straight Fork Ridge Trail. That trail terminates in two miles at FDR 237. Going right, and continuing downhill on the Devils Fork Trail, hikers return to the trailhead at four miles.

---

# Mount Rogers National Recreation Area

The 115,000-acre Mount Rogers National Recreation Area was established by Congress in 1966 to help take the pressure off Great Smoky Mountain and Shenandoah national parks. The "NRA" designation pledges these Jefferson National Forest lands to recreation and not the other "multiple uses" associated with the national forests, most notably the production of timber.

That's appropriate. This parcel of soaring property easily contains Virginia's most inspiring mountain scenery, not to mention the state's highest peak, Mount Rogers, at 5,729 feet. Whitetop Mountain, the state's second highest summit, sits nearby, and is the site of the state's loftiest motor road (State Route 89), a drive to spectacular and natural open meadows called "balds" in the South. There is also a fifty-five-mile loop (VA 603/US 58) of Mount Rogers, which is one of the few official U.S. Forest Service Scenic Byways in Virginia.

Virginia's highest state park, Grayson Highlands, sits on the flank of the National Recreation Area, and there are three national forest wilderness areas on the NRA; Lewis Fork, Little Wilson Creek, and Little Dry Run Wilderness.

Three hundred miles of trails, among them the Appalachian Trail, wind over that landscape. The area is highly scenic. Though covered by evergreens, many of Mount Rogers' radiating ridges are bare of trees, creating some of the most alpine scenery in the South. This "Crest Zone" is indeed spectacular, and trail users include horseback riders and cross-country skiers striding across nearly 100 inches of average annual snowfall. Trail destinations range from the popular High Country peaks, to quiet, seldom-visited valleys and beaver ponds.

Backup facilities include a wealth of developed recreation sites (also see the introduction to Grayson Highlands State Park). The NRA has six campgrounds (two open year round), six picnic areas, developed swimming sites and much, much more. The regular season for most facilities runs May to November.

Events include the Whitetop Maple Festival in late March that features a pancake feast, where you can sample the syrup. Call the local volunteer fire department and rescue squad for information, (703) 388-3422. There's also the Mount Rogers Naturalist's Rally in mid-May, a diverse series of seminars and guided hikes that explore the mountain's flora and fauna.

The area is far from major population centers, but relatively easy to reach. Interstate 81 parallels the NRA on the west, with access from Abingdon (exit 9), a sophisticated mountain village with upscale tourist facilities, Chilhowie (exit 13), and Marion (exit 16), the access point of choice if you want to stop at the NRA headquarters/visitor center, located seven miles from the interstate on VA 16 near Sugar Grove. Interstate 77 brings hikers to I-81 from the south. Ironically, residents of Tennessee and North Carolina find it easier to reach the mountain than many Virginians.

The NRA headquarters will send hikers a variety of brochures, a Sportsman's Map ($4.14), and USGS topo quads ($3 each Konnarock, Troutdale, and Whitetop Mountain are the maps for hikes listed in this book). The Mount Rogers High Country and Wildernesses Map is the one to have. It is available ($4.14), as are all of the above, from: Mount Rogers National Recreation Area, Route 1, Box 303, Marion, VA 24354, (540) 783-5196.

A variety of day and overnight hikes on Mount Rogers are described in separate entries, but the mountain certainly warrants a general introduction to other suggested hikes.

The truly long-distance hiker/backpacker will want to try the nearly forty-mile circuit that circles the entire area and includes a long stretch of the Iron Mountain Trail, a ridgetop trail north of Mount Rogers that used to be the Appalachian Trail. This circuit is covered on maps showing the Iron Mountain Trail/Whitetop-Laurel Loop, and the Mount Rogers Area Trails.

This route starts at the Mount Rogers National Recreation Trail (blue-blazed; see Mount Rogers and National Recreation Trail), heads right on the white-blazed Appalachian Trail at four miles, crosses Elk Garden Gap at six miles (VA 600), then crosses the summit of Whitetop Mountain and the crag of Buzzard Rock before reaching US 58 at fourteen miles.

The hike continues, with trestle crossings, on the old railroad grade of the Virginia Creeper Trail (see that entry) after the Appalachian Trail turns right.

At 21.4 miles, go right on a blue-blazed connector back to the A.T. and continue across US 58 and the Straight Branch parking area (at 23.5 miles) to the blue-blazed Feathercamp Trail at 23.6. At twenty-six miles, the yellow-blazed Iron Mountain Trail starts at the Sandy Flats shelter, and continues across FDR 90 at 26.1 miles to Straight Branch Shelter, at thirty-one miles. At thirty-two miles, go right .7 miles on the road to the trail's continuation on the crest. Reach the Cherry Tree Shelter at 36.5 miles. At thirty-seven miles turn right on the blue-blazed Flat Top Trail and descend back to the parking lot for the Mount Rogers Trail on VA 603.

That lengthy circuit is one of the best in the state, and can be longer and more scenic. To add scenic appeal and length, start at the Appalachian Trail parking area on VA 603, climbing past the Old Orchard Shelter and across spectacular Pine Mountain and Wilburn Ridge to the junction with the circuit described above. To return, just stay on the Iron Mountain Trail past the

Cherry Tree Shelter to the junction with the Appalachian Trail and descend to the parking area.

That circuit is just over forty-six miles, but could be substantially shortened on the less spectacular west end by taking the A.T. to the Beartree Recreation Area instead of the Virginia Creeper Trail. From the A.T., take the Beartree Gap Trail across US 58 to the purple-blazed trail up Grosses Mountain. At the crest, turn east on the Iron Mountain Trail, having shortened the loop by about ten miles.

You might also just focus on the scenic High Country area of Mount Rogers and make a 22.5 mile loop of Mount Rogers, Pine Mountain, and Iron Mountain. That would involve starting at the Appalachian Trail on VA 603 and crossing the Pine Mountain/Wilburn Ridge area, as described above. Then you would take a right on the Mount Rogers National Recreation Trail back down to VA 603. Ascend to Iron Mountain on the Flat Top Trail. Go north to the A.T. and back down to VA 603 for a circuit of the area's most alpine scenery.

Another nice option is the easy, 11.5-mile circuit of the Whitetop-Laurel Creek. The trip starts at the fishermen's parking lot, on the right, .25 mile up the Beartree Road from US 58. Take the Lake Shore Trail and turn right on the Beartree Gap Trail after crossing the dam and reach US 58 at .3 mile. Cross the road and turn right on the white-blazed Appalachian Trail at .6 mile.

At five miles turn left onto the Virginia Creeper Trail and follow through the isolated community of Taylor's Valley. Back at the A.T. junction (nine miles), hikers turn left to reach the Beartree Gap Trail (at eleven miles) and the parking area at 11.6 miles. Where the A.T. leaves the Virginia Creeper Trail, a 550-foot railroad trestle, now trail bridge, spans a gorge just .5 mile upstream on the way to a Virginia Creeper trailhead on State Route 728.

And these are just a few of the fine hikes in the Mount Rogers National Recreation Area.

# HIKE 3  THE VIRGINIA CREEPER NATIONAL RECREATION TRAIL

**General description:** A thirty-four-mile "rails to trails" conversion of the Norfolk and Western rail line between Abingdon, Virginia, and Whitetop Station on the Virginia/North Carolina state line. The easy grade, at times spectacular scenery and impressive trestles make the Virginia Creeper a fine option for hikers, as well as mountain bikers, horseback riders, and cross-country skiers.

**Elevation gain and loss:** Minimal, grade never more than five percent.

**Trailhead elevation:** Varies.

**High point:** 3,600 feet.

**Low point:** 1,900 feet.

**Water availability:** The trail parallels streams for most of its distance, but water is best picked up before hiking at any of the towns adjacent to trailheads.

**Finding the trailheads:** There are least fourteen trailheads along the trail. A handful are covered here.

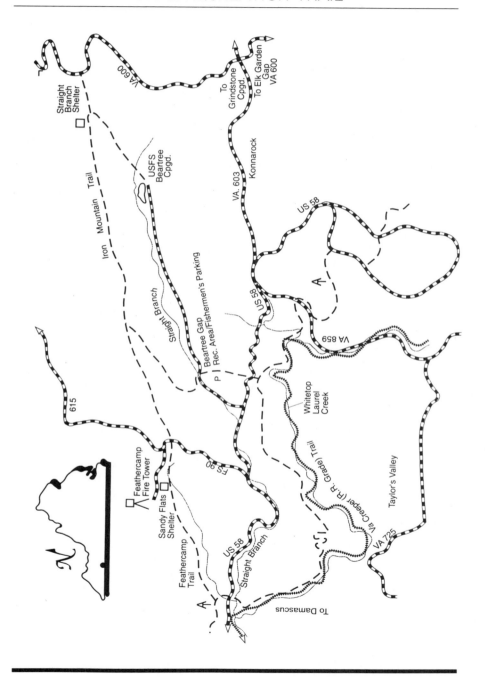

**The hike:** Most serious hikers seem to think that walking along an old railroad grade is pretty, well, dull. Perhaps it is on larger, placid streams, or in very urban areas when the walker would actually rather be in the wilderness. If that's what you want the Virginia Creeper may not be for you.

The Virginia Creeper is similar to, but different from many of those mundane railroad grade routes. In the vicinity of Abingdon, the South Holston River is a large stream, and the surrounding scenery is pastoral. But from Damascus "on up," the gradual route follows a tumbling wilderness stream that offers "world class" trout fishing. This upper section of the Virginia Creeper can be linked with the Appalachian Trail to provide an easy overnight backpacking circuit that's perfect for beginners (see Mount Rogers National Recreation Area).

Granted this isn't a guide to mountain biking and horseback riding, but since some hikers do both, keep those activities in mind for this trail. It adequately accommodates many uses.

Trestles on the river are impressive, and the surrounding scenery is wild, appropriate since the trail corridor was actually an Indian trace leading from North Carolina to the Ohio River, and the supposed site of four of Daniel Boone's campsites.

The trail "starts" in Abingdon, an historic mountain town that provides nice dining and lodging for hikers in the Mount Rogers area. The trailhead is downtown, near the corner of A Street SE and Green Springs Road. Find it by taking Pecan Street from Main Street. To reach Main Street, exit I-81 at exit 8 and go north on Alternate 58 to Main Street. Turn right, immediately pass the historic Martha Washington Inn and Barter Theater, and soon reach the right turn onto Pecan Street.

The trailhead is located where the old Indian trace of the Creeper Trail crossed another Native American travel route that ran up and down the Great Valley of Virginia. In pre-Revolutionary War times, the crossroads, and indeed the trailhead was occupied by Black's Fort, refuge for local settlers during an Indian raid in 1776. In 1778, the area became Abingdon, said to be "the first English speaking town on waters flowing to the Mississippi."

Today the site is a nice, small town trailhead. Nearby, stand the columns of Montcalm, the estate of David Campbell, governor of Virginia in 1837. A huge steam locomotive, engine 433, now sits on permanent display at the trailhead. The engine was among those that ran the "V-C" line, the Virginia-Carolina line that by 1900 reached Damascus. By 1905, the tracks had been extended to Konnarock (see entry for Mount Rogers National Recreation Trail), and would soon be carrying the virgin red spruce of the Mount Rogers area to market.

With those lumber trains in mind, it's easy to understand the nickname Virginia Creeper. The vine of that name also grows beside the tracks.

The railroad became the Norfolk and Western in 1918, and floods during the Great Depression spelled the end of its heyday. Ironically, the train ran weekly as far as West Jefferson, North Carolina, until 1976. The railroad sold the right of way to the towns of Abingdon, Damascus, and the U.S. Forest Service between the late 1970's and early 1980's. The trail was dedicated in 1987.

Today the path runs from Abingdon, where signs interpret the flora and audio tapes for use on the trail are available at the library, to Damascus, a town well-known as an Appalachian Trail re-supply and rest point. From there, the trail enters the Mount Rogers National Recreation Area and takes on a wilderness character not often found on a railroad grade trail.

From Abingdon, a nice 3.7-mile hike terminates at Watauga, reached southeast of Abingdon, and is located by taking U.S. 58 southeast from exit 9 of I-81, and then turning right on State Route 677 to the trailhead. That section of trail passes the home of Civil War veteran and Virginia Governor Wyndham Robertson, parallels Berry Creek with views of beaver dams, and then passes through a wooded, hilly area called the Great Knobs. There is one large trestle and pastoral scenery.

Damascus is the place to start sampling the wilder character of the trail. The trailhead sits beside a town park where U.S. 58 makes a sharp turn over the Beaver Dam Creek Bridge. An old steam engine used by the loggers sits at this site, as does the former Deep Gap trail shelter removed from the Appalachian Trail near the summit of Mount Rogers (see Mount Rogers National Recreation Trail).

To immediately start on the woodsy area of the trail, leave Damascus on US 58 east. After a straight drive through downtown, US 58 makes a sharp right at a junction with VA 91. The roads continue together to the edge of town, with the Virginia Creeper Trail on the right. Then U.S. 58 swings left and State Route 91 heads right. Measure driving distances to trailheads from that point.

There are many trailheads. But the ones mentioned here are located at (A) .9 miles, where U.S. 58 crosses a bridge, at (B) three miles, on U.S 58 at Straight Branch parking area (a trail crossing included in a circuit hike described under Mount Rogers National Recreation Area), and at (C) State Route 728, reached from U.S. 58, 8.8 miles from the measuring point, with a right onto State Route 728 to the trailhead. This latter trailhead is at the confluence of White Top Laurel and Green Cove Creeks, and also close to an easy backpacking circuit of the Whitetop Laurel Creek mentioned in the entry on the Mount Rogers National Recreation Area.

Starting at State Route 728 (parking area C), hikers can see the 550-foot Creek Junction Trestle just upstream. The bridge is really two trestles, and the A. T. branches left between them. You'll notice a monument to Hassinger, the timber baron who footed the rest of the bill for the fledgling railroad when the original builder, W. B. Mingea, ran out of money at this trestle. This elaborate bridge leaves little doubt as to why its construction became a stumbling block.

Downstream is the most scenic part of the trail, and the path is good enough to accommodate big-tired wheelchairs all the way to Damascus.

With one car, hikes from these trailheads are easy out and back walks. With two cars, lengthy and challenging one way hikes are possible. The easiest hikes are downhill. But remember, trail distances between the trailheads—labeled A, B, and C above—are different from the road mileages cited for reaching the parking areas. (Also be aware that the concrete mileage markers along the trail are .5 mile off: they are based on the location of the Abingdon train station, .5 mile farther into town than the trailhead.)

From Damascus, it is two miles on the Virginia Creeper Trail to parking area A on U.S. 58. From Parking area A to B, Straight Branch parking area, it is also two miles, or four miles from Damascus. From parking area B to C, it is 5.5 miles, or nine miles from Damascus, by trail.

Any hike you can devise up or downstream between parking lots A, B, and C is highly recommended. The 7.5 mile hike (fifteen miles round-trip) has outstanding streamside scenery, especially through the Whitetop Laurel Gorge/Taylor Valley area between parking areas B and C.

Camping is generally discouraged along the more pastoral parts of the trail between Abingdon and Damascus. In the national forest, camping is permitted, with the suggestion that overnighters camp well off the trail.

If you're reconnoitering the trail while in the Mount Rogers Area, or just want to sample the sights, check out the Creek Junction Trestle, and then go past parking lot C to the Green Cove trailhead (reached via U.S. 58, with a right turn onto VA 600 to the trailhead). The trailhead is the site of the only train station that remains from the days when the Virginia Creeper was hi-tech transportation for long-isolated Appalachian Mountaineers.

A former conductor inherited the building. It changed hands, and the Virginia Creeper Trail Club and U.S. Forest Service offered to renovate it. After it was refurbished, the owner donated it to the forest service. Now it recalls a long-gone era, and serves as a popular start for the Virginia Creeper Trail Club's mountain bike rides to Damascus (fifteen miles), and even back to Abingdon, thirty miles away.

For more information on the Virginia Creeper Trail, contact: The Virginia Creeper Trail Club, P.O. Box 2382, Abingdon, Virginia 24210; or Mount Rogers National Recreation Area, Route 1, Box 303, Marion, Virginia 24354, (540) 783-5196.

# HIKE 4  *MOUNT ROGERS NATIONAL RECREATION TRAIL*

**General description:** Virginia's highest summit, and three routes to reach it, including a strenuous National Recreation Trail hike of 6.7 miles (13.4 miles round-trip). A shorter, 4.2 mile (8.4-mile round-trip) route is moderately strenuous, starts at Grayson Highlands State Park and is described here and under the entry for Wilburn Ridge.
**Elevation gain and loss:** 3,998 feet.
**Trailhead elevation:** 3,730 feet.
**High point:** 5,729 feet.
**Water availability:** Water is available in season at Grindstone Campground, just west of the trailhead. It is available year round at the community of Konnaroc Gap, and near the new Thomas Knob Shelter.
**Finding the trailhead:** From Interstate 81, take exit 16, for VA 16 south to Troutdale, about seventeen miles. Turn right at Troutdale onto VA 603 and the trail begins in six miles on the left, with parking on the right.

**The hike:** The spruce-covered summit of Mount Rogers offers no view, just a summertime rarity in the South–fragrant, sun-dappled shade below cool evergreens. If that distinctive experience isn't enough, the three routes to the peak offer just about every other kind of scenery, including open, alpine-like meadows and some of the region's best views.

The first way described here to reach the peak starts on the Mount Rogers National Recreation Trail, a 4.5-mile, blue-blazed route that climbs through the Lewis Fork Wilderness. It starts at Grindstone Campground, the second largest campground in the Mount Rogers National Recreation Area.

The trail is graded, meaning natural soil has been moved to permit a consistent grade. It climbs in relatively gradual switchbacks, and advanced Nordic skiers can cross-country this often snowy, north-facing trail. The path rises through a hardwood forest of maples and beeches to birches and scattered spruce before dipping into Deep Gap and a junction with the Appalachian Trail at 4.5 miles.

Until the summer of 1992, Deep Gap was the site of Deep Gap Shelter, a facility that attracted large numbers of campers, usually from the high elevation Elk Garden Gap trailhead, just 1.9 miles away on VA 600. Because of damage resulting from overuse, the shelter was disassembled in summer 1992 and rebuilt as an information kiosk at the Virginia Creeper trailhead in Damascus, Virginia (see that entry). Camping has been prohibited in the area of the former shelter.

Taking a left on the white-blazed Appalachian Trail, the path rises, skirts a meadow, wanders through evergreens, and breaks out into open scenic views below the peak of Mount Rogers. At 6.2 miles, the blue-blazed Mount Rogers Spur Trail goes left from the A.T.. The side trail ascends through meadows, then enters dense evergreens and eventually winds its way through mossy rocks to the peak, at 6.7 miles. This, and a similar forest on Whitetop, are the only red spruce forests in the state.

The obvious excess of fallen trees on the .5-mile spur trail is the combined legacy of major ice storms in the mid-1980's, and the surprising force with which the remnants of Hurricane Hugo struck the area in 1989. This is also an area where research into what is popularly called "acid rain" is taking place. Depending on their species, the skeletal trees visible here, and at Whitetop, may be the victims of various kinds of air pollution, acid rain, and other forms of environmental stress. Among those stress factors, especially for the Fraser Fir that also grows at this altitude, is the Balsam Woolly Aphid, a pest brought into the U.S. in the early part of the century.

The Mount Rogers summit is a rarely visited place, but that might change. With the removal of the Deep Gap Shelter, the forest service and the local Appalachian Trail Club have erected a new shelter just beyond the left turn that takes hikers to the peak on the Mount Rogers Spur Trail. That location is a good one for many reasons, most notably that it is a better choice for an overnight campsite between Elk Garden Gap, and the next A.T. shelter, Old Orchard. Nevertheless, the new log shelter (and a nearby water source) places a developed camping facility close to a peak that was always insulated from popularity by distance and the need to carry a tent.

The next shortest distance to the summit, and probably the most scenic route, follows the Wilburn Ridge (see that entry) from Grayson Highlands State Park. That route reaches Rhododendron Gap in 2.5 miles, and continues on the A.T. through open meadows, past the newly constructed Thomas Knob Shelter, and reaches a right turn on the Mount Rogers Spur Trail at 3.7 miles. The entire hike to the summit is 4.2 miles (8.4 miles round-trip).

The shortest hike begins on VA 600, a connector between US 58 and VA 603 that climbs between Mount Rogers and Whitetop to Elk Garden Gap. The trailhead, at 4,434 feet, has ample parking and is situated in a large grassy

*From the peaks of Wilburn Ridge, the view from Mount Rogers stretches back toward the crags of Big Pinnacle in Grayson Highlands State Park.*

area, about 3.5 miles south of Konnarock, on VA 603, and another 3.5 miles north of the US 58/VA 603 junction.

The A.T. leaves the gap to the east and climbs over a bald knob with fine views of Mount Rogers black-capped summit. It reaches Deep Gap in 1.9 miles, and continuing on the Appalachian Trail, the hike reaches the Mount Rogers Spur Trail at 3.6 miles, and the summit at 4.1 miles (8.2 miles round-trip).

There are options on this last route. The Virginia Highlands Horse Trail starts at Elk Garden Gap also, and it skirts the first steep knob on the A.T. and climbs gradually to Deep Gap. The two choices are similar in distance, but the horse trail is much easier, and in winter, makes an excellent ski trail. The Deep Gap shelter, so often a lunch stop for skiers, no longer exists.

# Grayson Highlands State Park

Virginia's highest state park perches on the flank of Mount Rogers, the state's highest peak at 5,729 feet. This may be Virginia's most inspiring mountain scenery. The 5,000-acre state park boasts spectacular views of surrounding Jefferson National Forest land, including wilderness areas and the Mount Rogers National Recreation Area. There are nine hiking trails in the park, not all of which are covered here.

The park is located midway between Damascus and Independence, Virginia, and is reached from US 58. The entrance road, which begins at 3,698 feet, is 40.5 miles east of Abingdon, the location of I-81, and an historic valley town with distinctive dining and lodging. The entrance road is 7.5 miles east of Volney.

Grayson Highlands is one of the state's newest state parks, and has been warmly embraced by the isolated local communities of southwestern Virginia that surround it. A fall festival, held the last full weekend in September, often coincides with peak fall color and is a scenic and cultural attraction.

The park's developed facilities, which include a full-service campground (seventy-three sites, bathhouses), stables (twenty-four campsites, bathhouse), a picnic area (shelters by reservation, water, restrooms),and a visitor center (mountain culture museum, craft shop), which are open from late May to September.

At other times, especially in the winter, various park roads are gated, but access is always available to Massie Gap, a popular Appalachian Trail access point three miles from the entrance gate. This park is one of the best places

*Mount Rogers' mix of evergreens and open meadows creates one of the Old Dominion's most scenic hiking spots.*

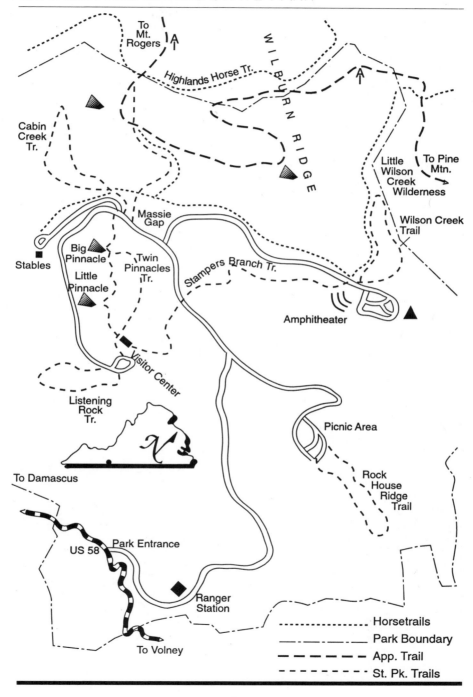

To Mt. Rogers

WILBURN RIDGE

Highlands Horse Tr.

Cabin Creek Tr.

Little Wilson Creek Wilderness

To Pine Mtn.

Wilson Creek Trail

Massie Gap

Stables

Big Pinnacle

Twin Pinnacles Tr.

Little Pinnacle

Stampers Branch Tr.

Amphitheater

Visitor Center

Listening Rock Tr.

N

Picnic Area

To Damascus

Rock House Ridge Trail

US 58    Park Entrance

Ranger Station

To Volney

| | |
|---|---|
| ·········· | Horsetrails |
| —·—·—·— | Park Boundary |
| — — — — | App. Trail |
| – – – – | St. Pk. Trails |

in the state for winter campers and cross-country skiers to easily reach snowy high elevation areas.

A modest parking fee is charged at the park gate year-round. Backpackers bound for nearby national forests must register for overnight parking; the park is a day use area and allows no backpack camping. Campground fees are charged. Sites may be reserved in advance year-round for an additional fee by phone or mail from Virginia State Parks Reservation Center, P.O. Box 1895, Richmond, Virginia, 23215-1815, (800) 933-7275, 9 a.m.-4 p.m., Monday through Friday, with check, money order, Visa or MC.

For more park information, contact: Grayson Highlands State Park, Route 2, Box 141, Mouth of Wilson, Virginia 24363, 703-579- 7092.

# HIKE 5 *MOUNT ROGERS' WILBURN RIDGE LOOP*

**General description:** An approximately five-mile loop from Grayson Highlands State Park over the Wilburn Ridge of Mount Rogers. This moderate day hike arguably traverses Virginia's most alpine scenery.
**Elevation gain and loss:** 1,700 feet.
**Trailhead elevation:** 4,680 feet.
**High point:** 5,530 feet.
**Map:** U.S. Forest Service "Mount Rogers High Country and Wildernesses."
**Water availability:** Available at developed state park facilities and at a spring near the high point.
**Finding the trailhead:** This hike begins at Massie Gap, the major trailhead parking area at Grayson Highlands State Park. The main road enters the park, climbs past a picnic area and campground and levels off opposite open meadows in Massie Gap .

**The hike:** The Wilburn Ridge area defies the stereotype of the rounded, tree-covered Appalachian summit. The general area of this walk serves up some of the South's most alpine, open scenery. This is one of very few meadow-covered mountaintops in Virginia.

In the South, these are called balds. Scientists haven't been able to explain the ones that appear natural. Though they look like alpine tundra areas that lie above the timberline in New England, the harsh climate is nevertheless not harsh enough for Mount Rogers to have a true treeline. Scientists speculate that the peak would need to be nearly 8,000 feet high to reach the weather conditions that would limit the growth of trees.

Most of the South's balds, those mysterious summit grasslands, are in neighboring North Carolina on 6,000-foot summits. Mount Rogers' meadows are likely the result of fire that erupted after part of this "crest zone" was logged in the early part of this century. After the towering virgin spruce forest was cut, the deep humus dried and caught fire. The Wilburn Ridge burned down to bare rock and mineral soil.

This loop hike ascends the Wilburn Ridge, a barren arm of Mount Rogers. This ridge contrasts sharply with the rounded, evergreen-covered bulge of the mountain's highest peak, visible nearby, and 200 feet higher.

The hike heads northwest of the plentiful parking spaces that line the road. Taking the state park's blue-blazed Rhododendron Trail, hikers cross the

*Wild ponies graze the meadows of Wilburn Ridge and Mount Rogers.*

park's access horse trail, slip through a fence stile, pass an orientation sign and head up the first large meadow.

This is airy country. Cool days can be cold here, and sudden weather changes can bring severe weather. On all but beautiful days, be prepared for alpine weather conditions.

At the crest of the first meadow, follow the Appalachian Trail's white blazes left toward open-horizon views of the craggy pinnacles that cap this soaring ridge. This area is woven with trails, so don't worry if you alternate between the different paths that angle toward the clump of evergreens below the major peak. At the evergreens, hikers cross a fence into the Mount Rogers National Recreation Area.

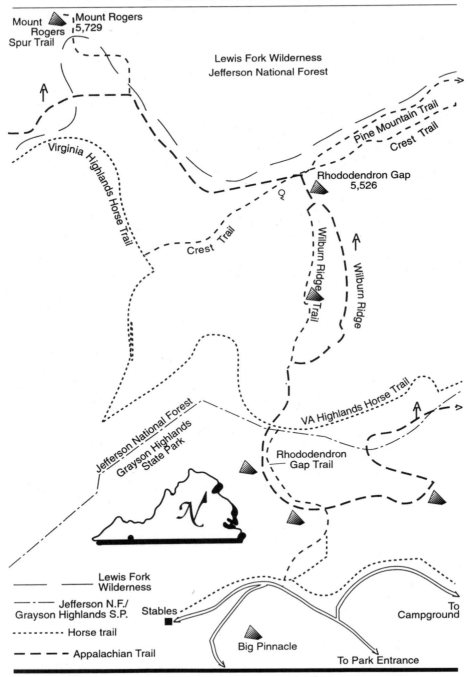

Mount Rogers
Mount Rogers Spur Trail

Mount Rogers 5,729

Lewis Fork Wilderness
Jefferson National Forest

Virginia Highlands Horse Trail

Pine Mountain Trail

Crest Trail

Rhododendron Gap 5,526

Crest Trail

Wilburn Ridge Trail

Wilburn Ridge

VA Highlands Horse Trail

Jefferson National Forest

Grayson Highlands State Park

Rhododendron Gap Trail

Stables

Big Pinnacle

To Campground

To Park Entrance

Lewis Fork Wilderness

Jefferson N.F./ Grayson Highlands S.P.

Horse trail

Appalachian Trail

During this first part of the hike, you're likely to see grazing ponies, singly and in groups. Like the wild horses on Chincoteague Island at the opposite end of the state, these little horses wander at will, and once a year a certain portion are rounded up by a private association and auctioned off. In this case, the grazing of the ponies is one of diverse methods used by the U.S. Forest Service to maintain the open character of the balds.

In winter, the ponies can inspire pity, huddled behind groves of shivering evergreens, hoarfrost matted in their manes. The ponies are shy, but don't attempt to feed them or they can become demanding. They have been known to find it difficult to differentiate between, for instance, a hot dog and a human finger.

The trail winds through the spruce groves, skirting ribs of rock and beautiful carpets of ferns. The peaks rise on the right, and the recently rerouted Appalachian Trail turns east and skirts to the right of the peaks on the way to Rhododendron Gap, where the ridge joins the larger bulk of Mount Rogers at about 2.5 miles. A spring lies off to the left of the trail. (Substantial human use and the presence of grazing animals make the purity of all spring and stream water suspect. Boil or treat chemically.)

The trip back, on the blue-blazed Wilburn Ridge Trail (FS Trail 4597), crosses the two major crags on the ridge, the first summit literally forming the southeastern side of Rhododendron Gap. The trail ascends to the peak through boulders, then descends, runs the meadow between the peaks, and scales the next, more massive summit.

Views from either peak are all-encompassing. Mount Rogers and White Top are nearby, and the expansive meadows of Pine Mountain sweep away to the northeast. South and west, the peaks of northwestern North Carolina's "High Country" rise, among them Grandfather Mountain. One rounded summit, with a nipple-like cap, is Sugar Mountain, topped by a ten story ski resort condo.

Just below, the ridges roll back to Grayson Highlands State Park, and craggy Haw Orchard Mountain, just across Massie Gap. Picnic spots beckon from sun-warmed, grassy nooks between boulders. The descent rejoins the Appalachian Trail, one mile from Rhododendron Gap, near the first grove of evergreens. Hikers just retrace their steps back to Massie. You may wish to take side trips to adjacent crags, on the right and left of the trail.

Under very deep snow, or after repeated storms, advanced Nordic skiers can actually tour this loop. Winter mountaineers should also keep this area in mind for real alpine adventure. The road to Massie Gap is well plowed after snowstorms, but winter visitors should take this area very seriously.

Autumn's crisp breezes and clear air seem to suit this hike best. Even in the direct sunlight of summer, this hike is nice, especially on the breezy peaks.

# HIKE 6 TWIN PINNACLES TRAIL

**General description:** This is a moderate, 1.6-mile interpretive nature loop over the highest summits in Grayson Highlands State Park. There are fine views of Mount Rogers, the state's highest peak.

**Elevation gain and loss:** Approximately 500 feet.

**Trailhead elevation:** 4,935 feet.

**High point:** 5,089 feet.

**Water availability:** Water is available at the trailhead visitor center, May to October.

**Finding the trailhead:** The trailhead is located on the southwest side of the Grayson Highlands State Park Visitor Center at the highest, most distant point on the state park road. The park entrance road is reached via US 58, midway between Independence and Damascus, Virginia.

**The hike:** Starting from the 4,935-foot elevation of the Grayson Highlands State Park Visitor Center, the Twin Pinnacles Trail is the easiest hike to mountaintop views in the Mount Rogers area.

The red-blazed trail climbs gradually to Little Pinnacle, 5,089 feet. Little Pinnacle is only .3 mile from the parking area, making this a worthwhile and easy walk for even the most sedentary visitor. Ten numbered posts correspond to an interpretive brochure, the first six stops of which are located between the trailhead and Little Pinnacle. The last four posts are between Little and Big Pinnacle.

The 360-degree view from Little Pinnacle includes surrounding crags and distant views of evergreen-covered Mount Rogers, Virginia's highest peak at 5,729 feet. Also visible is the meadow-covered summit of White Top, the state's second highest peak at 5,520 feet.

The trail then drops steeply into the gap that separates the Little Pinnacle from Big Pinnacle, .5 mile farther away. In the gap, the main trail loops right to the parking area, and a side trail heads left to the peak—a short, steep climb. On the way up, the Big Pinnacle Trail heads .4 mile down to Massie Gap, and the park road, a steep but useful route to the peak when snow requires gating the road to the visitor center.

From Big Pinnacle (5,068 feet), the massive, crag-capped meadows on Mount Roger's Wilburn Ridge appear almost-alpine. Views reach down to Massie Gap, and the drainage of the Little Wilson Creek Wilderness Area. Back at the gap, the trail loops back under Little Pinnacle, returning to the visitor center in an easy .8 mile.

Omitting the climb to Big Pinnacle creates a spectacular and easy loop hike with only one moderately steep descent. Two wooden rain shelters are located on the trail—one in the gap, one on the way back to the visitor center. The trail crosses rocky areas, and a few flights of stone steps, but much of the pathway is flat and grassy.

The vegetation on this trail is particularly interesting. Red spruce intermingle with spine-covered hawthorns, mountain ash, and yellow birches. Graceful ferns mix with mosses and ground cedar in the dampness under the trees. This is a strikingly picturesque northern-type forest. Where crags rise out of the stunted trees, the scene is reminiscent of timberline on much higher mountains.

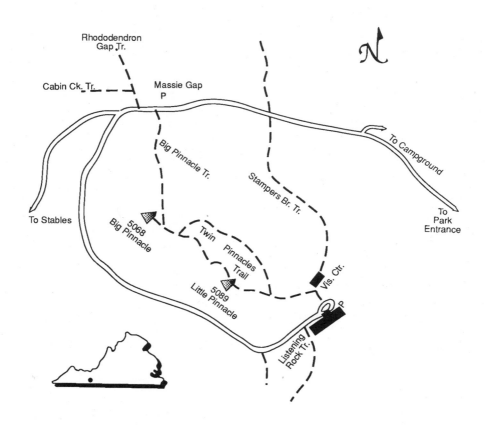

# HIKE 7 *CABIN CREEK TRAIL*

**General description:** A moderate two-mile loop in Grayson Highlands State Park that is a perfect streamside hike for fall.

**Elevation gain and loss:** 560 feet.

**Trailhead elevation:** 4,640 feet.

**Low point:** 4,360 feet.

**Water availability:** Trail follows Cabin Creek—boil or treat water taken from the creek. Clean water available at park facilities.

**Finding the trailhead:** Park at the main Massie Gap trailhead in Grayson Highlands State Park, opposite the meadows of the Wilburn Ridge.

**The hike:** From Massie Gap, head for the meadows of Wilburn Ridge, but bear left along the edge of the paved road that leads down to the state park's fine stable facility.

The swale between Massie Gap and the evergreen/rhododendron forest is a beautiful, alpine-like meadow. Entering the woods, the unblazed trail winds through an intimate, over-arching forest of Rosebay rhododendron to a stream crossing. In this vicinity , pioneer Lee Massey and his family, the namesake of Massie Gap, had a cabin in the late 1800s.

Take the left fork at the split, and descend in half a mile to Cabin Creek. The trail follows the stream, soon ascending the edge of a striking waterfall. When the trail switchbacks to the right and leaves the stream, the hike follows a level logging grade all the way back to the junction. (Cross-country skiers could make this top section a nearly two-mile out-and-back ski tour. They, or hikers wanting a flat walk, should take a right at the first junction.)

This is a great autumn stroll, in part because the colorful trees along the trail include yellow birches and big-toothed aspens, the latter a rarity in Virginia. Other colorful species contrast with the Fraser fir and red spruce.

---

## Hungry Mother State Park

# HIKE 8 
### HUNGRY MOTHER STATE PARK AND HIKING TRAILS

---

**General description:** A legend-rich state park near Marion, Virginia, with more than twelve miles of easy to strenuous hiking.
**Elevation gain and loss:** Approximately 1,940 feet.
**Trailhead elevation:** Approximately 2,300 feet.
**High point:** Approximately 3,270 feet.
**Water availability:** Water is available Monday through Friday year-round at the park office, and during the summer at the park's many developed facilities. Also, just across the road from Campground A is a private business, the Camper's Quick Stop, that is open year-round.
**Finding the trailheads:** Hungry Mother State Park is four miles north of Marion on VA 16. To get there, take exit 17 on I-81, and go about a mile into Marion on U.S. 11. Turn right on VA 16 to the park.
**For more information:** Hungry Mother State Park, Route 5, Box 109, Marion, VA 24354, (540) 783-3422.

**The hike:** The oddly named Hungry Mother State Park is a 2,215-acre park near Marion. The park's name comes from a legendary incident that is probably true in one form or another. Hundreds of years ago, when Indians destroyed a few local settlements near the New River, Molly Marley and her small child were taken hostage and moved north to the raider's base camp. They eventually escaped, and made their way home fighting starvation. When Molly collapsed due to hunger, her tiny child made her way downstream, found help, and was only able to say "Hungry, Mother." At the foot of the mountain where she collapsed, the searchers found Molly dead. Hikers can walk the same stream and climb the peak where Molly was found, now named Molly's Knob.

## HUNGRY MOTHER STATE PARK AND HIKING TRAILS

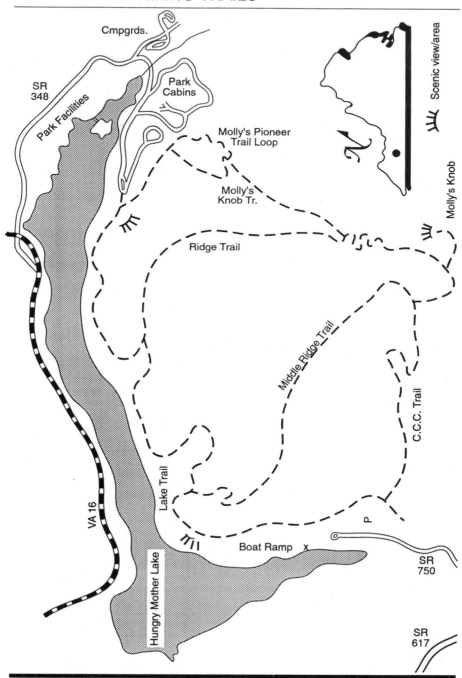

Cmpgrds.

SR 348

Park Facilities

Park Cabins

Molly's Pioneer Trail Loop

Molly's Knob Tr.

Ridge Trail

Middle Ridge Trail

C.C.C. Trail

Lake Trail

Hungry Mother Lake

VA 16

Boat Ramp    x

P

SR 750

SR 617

Scenic view/area

Molly's Knob

The park's centerpiece is a 108-acre lake noted for Virginia's best Northern Pike fishing. The last two state record fish were caught here, the biggest being nearly twenty-eight pounds.

Like some other of Virginia's best state parks, Hungry Mother was among the original six that were built in the 1930s largely through the labor of the Civilian Conservation Corps. The park's log visitor center, recently restored, was built by the CCC as a lodge. Five log cabins that are now available for rent were also built by the CCC. The park also has eight frame and seven concrete cabins. The park's restaurant, another CCC classic, overlooks the lake.

The park offers a public swimming beach on the lake, a forty-three-site campground, camp store, picnic areas (including three shelters available for rent by reservation). There is a boat launch area, and rowboats and paddle boats are for rent. Horses are also for rent during the Memorial Day to Labor Day summer season.

Hungry Mother stands out from other state parks for its Hemlock Haven Conference Center. The thirty-five-acre site was once a private inholding in the park. The original facilities were built in 1947, and then purchased and operated by the Virginia Episcopal Diocese in 1957. A pool, tennis courts, and a meeting facility were added, but in 1986, when upkeep became a problem for the church, the state bought the complex. In 1989, the renovated and expanded conference center opened. There are five small meeting rooms and one large hall that will hold up to 240 people for a meeting and up to 375 for a reception.

The center has five cabins and six lodges for guests. The pool, tennis courts, and sports facilities are also reserved for users of the meeting facility.

A parking fee is charged, as are camping fees. Sites may be reserved in advance (additional fee) in person at state parks and Ticket Master outlets, and by phone or mail at the Ticket Master Reservation Center, (804) 490-3939, 9 a.m.-5 p.m., Monday through Friday: money order, Visa, MC.

Trails in the park are located in two separate areas. A smaller cluster of paths lie north of the park restaurant, and the bulk of the trail system lies south of the lake in the vicinity of Molly's Knob. The Molly's Knob area trails are described separately, but the loop options are diverse.

## Raider's Run/Old Shawnee Trail

These two trails form two moderate loops that can be combined. Park in parking lot 2 across from the park restaurant and enter the blue-blazed Raider's Run Trail. This wide path, formerly a horse trail, loops gradually up to a junction with the Old Shawnee Trail. Raider's Run is a particularly nice wildflower walk in the spring. Just the Raider's Run loop is 1.5 miles.

The white-blazed Old Shawnee Trail (one mile) loops away from the Raider's Run Trail and ascends to steeper ground. This trail is a narrower path that climbs to forest service property and crosses the wooded top of thirty foot cliffs, with views into a forested hollow. The outer loop of both trails is approximately a two-mile walk.

## The Molly's Knob Trail

The strenuous Molly's Knob Trail reaches Molly's Knob (1.6 miles, 3.2 miles round trip), the park's high point at about 3,270 feet. The last part of the climb is steep, but great southwestern Virginia views are the reward.

Hikers can see Mount Rogers, the state's highest peak, its neighbor Whitetop, the park's lake, the town of Marion, and much more.

The white-blazed trail starts from the park visitor center and follows part of Molly's Pioneer Trail, an interpretive trail closed for renovation until 1993. (The easy .6-mile loop tells about the life of early settlers.) Switchbacks mark the middle of the Molly's Knob Trail, and then the trail becomes steeper and hikers reach a junction on the right with the Ridge Trail. Beyond that, the trail becomes steeper, reaches a junction to the right with the CCC Trail, and then veers steeply upward to the summit.

## The Lake Trail

This easy, blue-blazed lakeshore trail (3.1 miles, 6.2 miles round trip) is a nice stroll for families. It, and a few side trails, permit more energetic hikers to create more strenuous loop hikes to Molly's Knob.

The trail starts at a sign at a turn-around/view on the road to the park visitor center. Park at the visitor center and walk the roadside to the sign and a nice view of the lake and beach. The road-width trail slides above the lake with good views, then dips into a hollow to meet the bottom of the Ridge Trail, .6 mile.

The trail becomes narrower, returns to the lake, and reaches a nice view from the top of a small cliff above the lake. It again dips back into a hollow to meet the start of the Middle Ridge Trail (2.1 miles from the parking area). The trail again swings out to the lake, with a nice view from a rise, and then turns southeast toward its terminus near the boat ramp, about 3.1 miles from the start.

Hikers could spot a car here to avoid an out-and-back hike. To do so, take a right turn onto state route 617 at the boat ramp sign, on the way to the park from Marion. About a mile later, make a left onto State Route 750 at a boat ramp sign and reach the ramp parking area in another .25 mile.

The CCC Trail also begins at this boat ramp parking area, allowing all of the extensive loops described next to begin here as well as at the visitor center.

## The CCC Trail

The orange-blazed CCC Trail (one mile) leaves the Lake Trail in the vicinity of the boat ramp. Access the Lake Trail from the edge of the parking area (no motorized vehicles sign) and follow it southeast into the woods around a small wetland to a signed junction with the CCC Trail near an old campground bathhouse.

The CCC Trail climbs gradually along a stream, steeply switchbacks, then becomes a gradual grade to its junction, at about .8 mile, with the Middle Ridge Trail. It terminates at one mile with the Molly's Knob Trail.

The large loop formed by the Molly's Knob, CCC, and Lake trails is a diverse, moderately strenuous hike of 5.7 miles. Smaller loops can be formed from either parking area by using the Middle Ridge and Ridge trails.

## The Middle Ridge Trail

A moderate, yellow-blazed 1.1-mile trail that climbs gradually from the Lake Trail to the CCC Trail.

## The Ridge Trail

A moderate, .7-mile gold-blazed trail that climbs from the Lake Trail to Molly's Knob Trail.

## Circuit Hike Options

These trails offer a variety of options. From the visitor center, a loop of the Molly's Knob, Ridge, and Lake trails is just under four miles. Also from the visitor center, a loop of the Molly's Knob, Middle Ridge, top of the CCC, and Lake Trails is about five miles.

From the boat ramp, a loop of the Lake, Middle Ridge, and CCC trails is just under three miles, and just under four miles if you include the summit of Molly's Knob. Also from the boat ramp, a loop of the Lake, CCC, Ridge, and Molly's Knob trails is about five miles. From either trailhead, the outer loop is about 5.7 miles.

*Small visual pleasures are hidden beneath the thick understory of southwestern Virginia forests.*

# Mountain Lake Wilderness

# HIKE 9 WAR SPUR TRAIL AND APPALACHIAN TRAIL

**General description:** Easy (1.5, 2.5 miles) to moderate and strenuous (five, seven, and nine miles) hikes near Blacksburg through one of Virginia's most spectacular wilderness areas. A variety of easy to moderate trails open to the public at Mountain Lake Hotel are also included here. See the hotel information at the end of this entry for those hikes.

**Elevation gain and loss:** War Spur Trail, 600 feet; Appalachian Trail, 2,472 feet.

**Trailhead elevations:** War Spur Trail, 3,700 feet; Appalachian Trail, 3,972 feet.

**High points:** War Spur Trail, 3,780 feet; A.T. 4,128 feet.

**Low points:** War Spur Trail, 3,560; A.T., 2,080 feet.

**Water availability:** Water is available year-round at the Mountain Lake Hotel, 5.5 miles south of the A.T. trailhead, and on the way to both trails. Water is available on the War Spur Trail from War Spur Branch, and on the A.T. from a spring at War Spur Shelter.

**Finding the trailheads:** To reach Mountain Lake Wilderness, take U.S. 460 west from Blacksburg to VA 700, about two miles past the town of Newport. Take VA 700 for about seven miles to the crest of the mountain and scenic Mountain Lake. Then take State Route 613 (the Salt Sulphur Turnpike), a road that becomes gravel and passes the University of Virginia Biological Research Station. Both trailheads are on the right: War Spur about 3.5 miles past Mountain Lake; the A.T. about 5.5 miles past.

**The hikes:** The roughly 11,000-acre Mountain Lake Wilderness area gets its name from Mountain Lake, a twenty-five-acre gem of a mountain pond that sits at 3,875 feet just east of the West Virginia state line. This is the only natural mountain lake in the state. The evergreen-highlighted setting is very reminiscent of New England, especially with the rambling old Mountain Lake Hotel perched on the shore.

The federal wilderness is five miles past the lake and the 2,600 acres of resort-owned land that surround it. The parcel of wildland occupies the Eastern Continental Divide. The headwaters of John's Creek and Little Stony Creek flow in different directions and eventually wind up in the Gulf of Mexico and the Atlantic, respectively.

The climate and vegetation of the area is similar to areas much farther north. The cool summer and snowy winter weather is very conducive to the growth of spruce, hemlock, and rhododendron. The area boasts a rare, and large, high mountain bog, an impressive, easily reached stand of virgin timber and a human history that includes significant troop movements during the Civil War.

Animals that roam the mature forests and cliff-laced area include bear, beaver, deer, bobcat, and snowshoe hare. The latter is a native, but re-introduced, species that indicates why the resort, and the wilderness is popular with cross-country skiers and winter visitors.

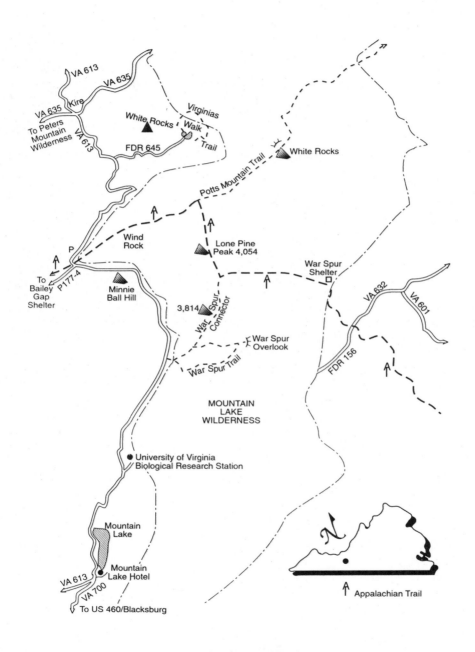

VA 613

VA 635

VA 635  Kire

To Peters
Mountain
Wilderness

VA 613

White Rocks

Virginias
Walk

FDR 645

Trail

Potts Mountain Trail

White Rocks

Wind
Rock

Lone Pine
Peak 4,054

War Spur
Shelter

P

To
Bailey
Gap
Shelter

P177-4

Minnie
Ball Hill

3,814

War Spur
Connector

War Spur
Overlook

VA 632

VA 601

FDR 156

War Spur Trail

MOUNTAIN
LAKE
WILDERNESS

University of Virginia
Biological Research Station

Mountain
Lake

Mountain
Lake Hotel

VA 613

VA 700

To US 460/Blacksburg

N

Appalachian Trail

*Virgin hemlock trees tower above hikers on the War Spur Trail in the Mountain Lake Wilderness.*

Efforts to preserve the unique area began formally in 1960 with the establishment of an approximately 1,500-acre Scenic Area by the forest service. Wilderness preservationists achieved Congressional designation of the tract as Wilderness in 1984, ten years after the Scenic Area had become a Wilderness Study Area.

The Appalachian Trail winds through the Wilderness, and an adjacent loop hike explores the virgin timber. Both trails offer good views.

The white-blazed Appalachian Trail is an "end-to-end" way to pass through the wilderness, requiring two cars to achieve an approximately five-mile hike or backpacking trip that can include a stay at War Spur Shelter.

The A.T. starts about 5.5 miles past Mountain Lake and climbs in a .25 mile to Wind Rock, the area's best long-range view. This view, mostly to the north, is a nice .5-mile, round-trip leg-stretcher.

The trail crosses the summit of Potts Mountain. A side trail runs northeast along the crest of that mountain. But follow the A.T. south, across Lone Pine Peak, to a junction with the War Spur Connector, about three miles from the start of the hike. This is a side trail to State Route 613, about 1.5 miles away, and the War Spur Loop (see the next trail description).

The A.T. starts a serious descent after this junction, actually a continuation of the nearly 2,000-foot drop from Lone Pine Peak to the next trailhead on FDR 156. This descent is the major recommendation for hiking south to north on the A.T. The War Spur Shelter is just off the trail, slightly over four miles from the start. Hiking .8 miles further north, hikers reach FDR 156.

To reach FDR 156, turn right on VA 42 from U.S. 460 in Newport, then turn left on State Route 658 near Simmonsville, about ten miles north of Newport. Take State Route 658 to a T-junction with State Route 632. Turn left on State Route 632 and continue after it becomes FDR 156.The trailhead is located on the right, about four miles from the junction.

The War Spur/Chestnut Trail loop offers an approximately 2.5-mile hike to a viewpoint that can be extended with a side trip on a connector to the Appalachian Trail. The link also makes an A.T./War Spur hike possible, with or without two cars.

This loop is the easiest introduction to the Mountain Lake Wilderness. The trail leaves State Route 613 about 3.5 miles beyond Mountain Lake. The entire circuit is easy. The recommended route bears right following the Chestnut Trail on the forest service's photocopy map of the area. The trail wanders out the ridge called War Spur to a side trail, reached at about one mile. The path leads right .25 mile to the John's Creek Overlook, a vista that includes much of the wilderness area.

Back at the junction, continue right, descending into the valley of War Spur Branch. Massive hemlocks cluster near the stream. Beyond the stand of virgin timber, hikers reach a junction at about the two-mile mark. A left reaches the parking area in about .5 mile, for a roughly 2.5-mile hike.

A right leads along the beautiful War Spur Connector to the Appalachian Trail, just under a mile away. The path is inspiringly parklike; grassy, and lined in summer with lush ferns. Taking this side trip to the A.T.; the round-trip back to your car is about 4.5 miles.

Incorporating most of the War Spur loop into a connection to the A.T., and an A.T. hike past Wind Rock, the total hike is about seven miles in either direction. You might avoid the need for two cars with a two-mile roadside walk between trailheads, undertaken at the start of a roughly nine-mile day hike.

Virginia's Nature Trail is an easy 1.5-mile trail that leads in a loop from the White Rocks forest service campground, very near the Mountain Lake Wilderness. The path wanders back and forth across the state line between Virginia and West Virginia. To reach the trail, go north from the A.T. Trail crossing on State Route 613 for just under 1.5 mile. Turn on FDR 645 and the campground is one mile.

Besides the campground, hikers might consider the Mountain Lake Hotel for accommodations. A lakeshore trail and other paths make the resort a very outdoorsy destination in its own right. The dining and lodging at the resort are upscale, but rooted in the hotel's status as a classic Southern Appalachian hostelry. For hotel details, contact: The Mountain Lake Hotel, Mountain Lake, Virginia 24136, (800) 346-3334.

Hotel guests and responsible members of the general public can use a variety of nice trails at the hotel. The easy Indian Trail circles the lake in about 1.7 miles. The moderate Jungle Trail makes a lengthier loop of the lake, about five miles, and includes a portion of trail across State Route 613 from the hotel. (This trail includes short stretches of road.) A great view is available on the Bald Knob Trail, which climbs about 500 vertical feet to the open summit of Bald Knob (4,363 feet) in a bout .7 mile.

All the trails start in the vicinity of the hotel (see the Cascades Trail Map for general trailhead location). Trail maps are available at the hotel.

Cross-country skis are not rented at the hotel during the winter, but much of the War Spur Loop is skiable, especially the connector to the Appalachian Trail. The hotel also has many skiable trails.

## Cascades National Recreation Trail

# HIKE 10   *THE CASCADES*

**General description:** An easy and very scenic two-mile (four-mile round trip) day hike to one of Virginia's most impressive waterfalls.
**Elevation gain and loss:** Approximately 1,340 feet.
**Trailhead elevation:** Approximately 2,140 feet.

*A gradual trail along Little Stony Creek leads to the Cascades, near Blacksburg, Virginia.*

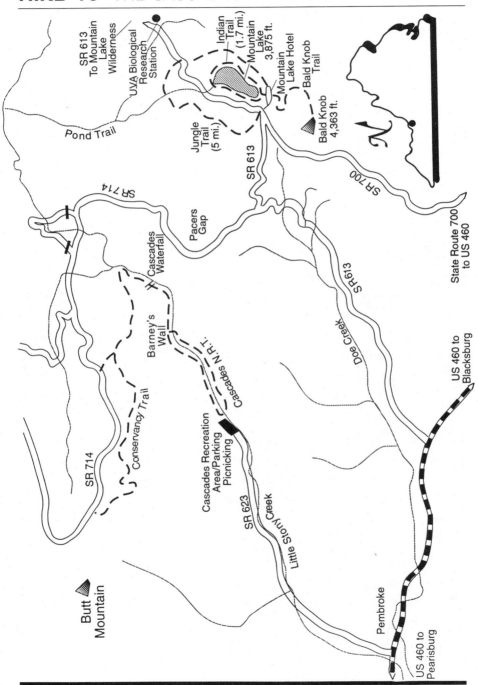

SR 613
To Mountain Lake Wilderness

UVA Biological Research Station

Indian Trail (1.7 mi.)

Mountain Lake 3,875 ft.

Mountain Lake Hotel

Bald Knob Trail

Bald Knob 4,363 ft.

Pond Trail

Jungle Trail (5 mi.)

SR 613

SR 700

State Route 700 to US 460

SR 714

Pacers Gap

Cascades Waterfall

Barney's Wall

Cascades N.R.T.

Conservancy Trail

SR 714

Doe Creek

SR 613

Cascades Recreation Area/Parking Picnicking

SR 623

Little Stony Creek

US 460 to Blacksburg

Butt Mountain

Pembroke

US 460 to Pearisburg

**High point:** Approximately 2,810 feet.

**Water availability:** Water is available in season at the trailhead facilities in the picnic area, and year round in the village of Pembroke, about 3.5 miles southwest.

**Finding the trailhead:** Take U.S. 460 west from Blacksburg, Virginia, about 17.5 miles to Pembroke. Signs there direct hikers to Cascades Recreation Area; take a right turn onto State Route 623 and reach the parking area in under four miles.

**The hike:** The Cascades is a justifiably popular hike, designated a National Recreation Trail. The well-marked path winds up Little Stony Creek, a fine trout stream, to a sixty-foot waterfall. The Cascades drops over a precipitous ledge into a deep pool, a favorite spot to cool off after the easy hike up.

The trail starts at the Cascades Recreation Area, a developed picnic area that in season offers picnicking facilities, drinking water, and toilets. The stream is a popular spot for trout fishing. This hike combines a fire road with portions of trail that stay close to, and occasionally use spans to cross, the rushing mountain stream. No camping is permitted at the recreation area, along the stream, or at The Cascades.

The hike starts where a wide valley narrows into a steep ravine. On the way up the creek, the increasingly steep walls of the adjoining mountains close-in, creating a cleft that rises from 1,000 to 1,500 feet on both sides of the stream. Views reach up to rocky outcrops on Barney's Wall, the left side of the ravine on the way up.

The 4,000-foot plateau above the cliffs is part of the climatologically unique Mountain Lake area (see that entry). The weather and vegetation on the crest is more like areas much farther north. Some of that filters down to the head of the Cascades Canyon, creating a cool crease where rhododendron cluster beneath lacy hemlocks.

At the head of the cleft, the Cascades sprays over a sharp drop-off and plummets into a pool that is hemmed-in by cliffs. It is cool here even on a hot day in the valley. In winter, the frozen waterfall and snowy trail are even more impressive.

# HIKE 11 *DRAGON'S TOOTH*

**General description:** The Dragon's Tooth is a rock formation on the Appalachian Trail that packs beautiful views into hikes of three, 4.2, and 4.6 miles.

**Elevation gain and loss:** 2,600 feet.

**Trailhead elevation:** About 1,750 feet.

**High Point:** 3,050 feet.

**Water availability:** The Catawba Grocery, on the left about .25 mile before the Dragon's Tooth trailhead, gladly permits hikers to fill canteens year round.

**Finding the Trailhead:** From Interstate 81 south of Roanoke, take exit 41 and go north on VA 311 about ten miles. The Dragon's Tooth trailhead is on the left, about .25 mile past the Catawba Grocery.

**The hike:** Dragon's Tooth is the turn-around point for a variety of spectacular, moderately strenuous hikes. There are a number of ways to hike this trail,

*Rhododendron blooms in June among the hardwoods and evergreens of Virginia's highest peaks.*

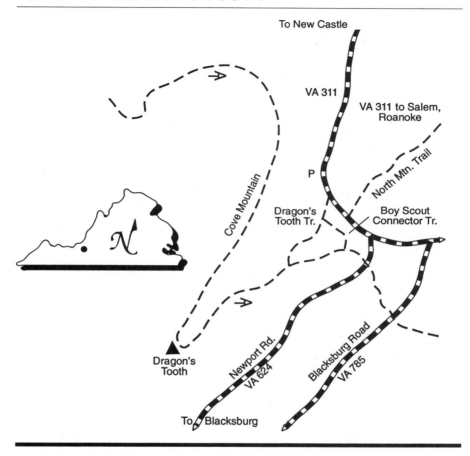

actually a portion of the Appalachian National Scenic Trail. Hikers can hike out and back on the Appalachian Trail by taking a left on State Route 624, and parking at that trailhead about a half mile from VA 311. That hike is 2.1 miles to Dragon's Tooth (4.2 miles round trip).

The Dragon's Tooth trailhead, and the start of the Appalachian Trail are both at about the same elevation, so the advantage of parking at the Dragon's Tooth trailhead is the existence of a trail loop on that side of the ridge. That permits hikers to include the loop in the longer hike to Dragon's Tooth, or create an even shorter option that doesn't include "the tooth" itself, but nevertheless crosses rocky crags with striking views in about three miles.

At 2.5 miles from the Dragon's Tooth parking area, hikers encounter a trail junction and trail information board. To the left the blue-blazed Boy Scout Trail climbs steeply to the Appalachian Trail, reaching it .5 mile from the parking area. To the right, the blue blazed Dragon's Tooth Trail gradually climbs a stream drainage through rhododendron and tall tulip poplar trees.

This trail reaches the A.T. about 1.5 miles from the parking lot.

Between the two trails, the white-blazed Appalachian Trail traverses a knife-edge ridgetop with various rocky viewpoints. By hiking up the more gradual Dragon's Tooth Trail, and then following the one mile section of the A.T. to the Boy Scout Trail, you can create a moderate three mile circuit hike. That same circuit can become part of the longer hike to Dragon's Tooth.

From Lost Spectacles Gap, where the Dragon's Tooth Trail intersects with the Appalachian Trail, the A.T. ascends crags and ledges to the peak of Cove Mountain (3,020 feet), then turns sharply right and follows the prominent ridgeline to the north. A blue-blazed side trail juts left to the Dragon's Tooth, a fanglike projection with fine views.

The tooth is about .8 mile from the junction with the Dragon's Tooth Trail, or 2.3 miles from the parking area. That's a 4.6-mile round trip hike, whether you include the loop or retrace your steps. More energetic hikers can extend this walk by as much as another three or four miles by continuing out the scenic crest of Cove Mountain.

# HIKE 12 *NORTH MOUNTAIN TRAIL*

**General description:** The North Mountain Trail is a 13.2 mile ridgetop walk that makes a nice overnight backpacking trip with two cars.
**Elevation gain and loss:** 2,900 feet.
**Trailhead elevation:** About 1,750 feet.
**High Point:** 3,200 feet.
**Water availability:** The Catawba Grocery, on the left about .25 mile before the Dragon's Tooth trailhead, gladly permits hikers to fill canteens year round.
**Finding the trailhead:** From Interstate 81 south of Roanoke, take exit 41 and go north on VA 311 about ten miles to the trailheads. The North Mountain trailhead is on the right, .2 past the junction with State Route 624, and before the Dragon's Tooth Trail.

**The hike:** Like the Iron Mountain Trail near Mount Rogers, Virginia's highest peak, the North Mountain Trail used to be a part of the Appalachian Trail. However, when the A.T. was rerouted, the once-popular route across North Mountain didn't cease to exist. Today, the 13.2-mile North Mountain Trail is a quiet ridgetop backpacking trip for campers with two cars.

The now yellow-blazed trail leaves a small parking area on VA 311, passes a signboard, and switchbacks steeply one mile to the ridgetop, approximately 2,900 feet. The trail undulates over peaks and crags, passing junctions with the Deer Trail at 2.4 miles (descends to FDR 224 in 1.6 miles), the Grouse Trail at 3.4 miles (descends to FDR 224 in 1.5 miles), and the Turkey Trail at just over six miles (descends to FDR 224 in 1.7 miles).

The old A.T. veers right off the ridge at nine miles, and the North Mountain Trail continues, gradually dropping to FDR 183 at just over thirteen miles. The easier climb of the trail leads south from this trailhead, reached just south of New Castle. Coming from the VA 311 trailhead, drive north past the Dragon's Tooth trailhead and turn right on FDR 224, passing all the side trailheads mentioned above. Turn right when FDR 224 intersects State Route 618, and continue until the road becomes FDR 183 and reaches the trailhead on the right.

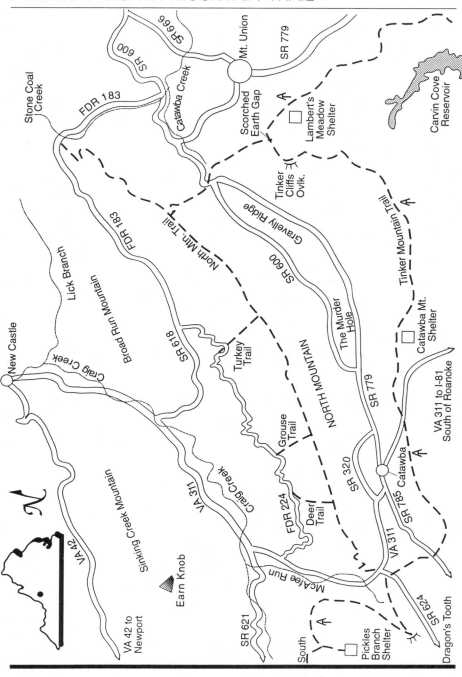

# Hoop Hole, Roaring Run National Recreation Trails

## HIKE 13 — HOOP HOLE TRAIL, ROARING RUN TRAIL, IRON ORE TRAIL

**General description:** Three intersecting loop trails north of Roanoke, and south of Covington, that offer hikes of 1.5, four, and nine miles.

**Elevation gain and loss:** 4,560 feet for Hoop Hole, 720 for Roaring Run.

**Trailhead elevation:** 1,320 feet for Hoop Hole; 1,160 for Roaring Run.

**High point:** 3,600 for Hoop Hole, 1,520 for Roaring Run.

**Water availability:** All of these trails start out on streams. The Roaring Run Furnace picnic area has pit toilets. Year-round flush toilets and a source of drinking water are now under construction, but finalized facilities are uncertain at this time. Check with the New Castle Ranger District (see Virginia National Forests). A store at the junction of VA 615/621 is a year-round source of water and supplies.

**Finding the trailheads:** From Interstate 81 just north of Roanoke, take exit 44 and go north on US 220 about fifteen miles to Eagle Rock. At Eagle Rock, turn left on VA 615 and go eight miles to the Hoop Hole trailhead on the right. To reach the Roaring Run Trail and picnic area, also take VA 615 from Eagle Rock, but turn right onto VA 621 at six miles. You will reach the picnic area and trailhead on VA 621 just over a mile from the turnoff.

**The hike:** The Hoop Hole double loop trail, the Roaring Run loop trail, and the Iron Ore Trail that links them, offer a wide variety of hikes, and even backpacking, in the general area of the Roaring Run picnic area.

These are all national recreation trails, a designation that promises high standards of scenery and maintenance. Unfortunately, the budget cuts of recent years haven't allowed the forest service to deliver on the improvements envisioned when the Hoop Hole and adjacent trails were proposed as NRT's. Nevertheless, this area is worth a visit.

The easiest trail, the Roaring Run Trail loop, is a 1.5 mile-long, graded, very developed trail that crosses five bridges as it follows a bold mountain stream. The trail begins in the picnic area and climbs through an impressive forest of hemlocks to a twenty-five-foot-high umbrella waterfall. On the way back from the falls, hikers should take a left, cross the stream and descend back to the start of the hike on the other side of the loop trail.

Near the parking area, across the creek from the start of the trail, the path passes the stone ruins of a pre-Civil War iron furnace, one of many visible at recreation areas in Virginia national forests.

The Hoop Hole Trail loop starts about 3.5 miles away and makes two loops on its climb to a high point near the summit of Rich Patch Mountain, 3,704 feet. The parking area on VA 615 is signed, and there is a nice routed trail map near the trailhead. A reasonable hiking map of the area is available free from the Newcastle Ranger District (see Virginia National Forests for ordering information).

The moderate lower loop is the best maintained at this writing. Whichever

# HIKE 13 *HOOP HOLE TRAIL, ROARING RUN TRAIL, IRON ORE TRAIL*

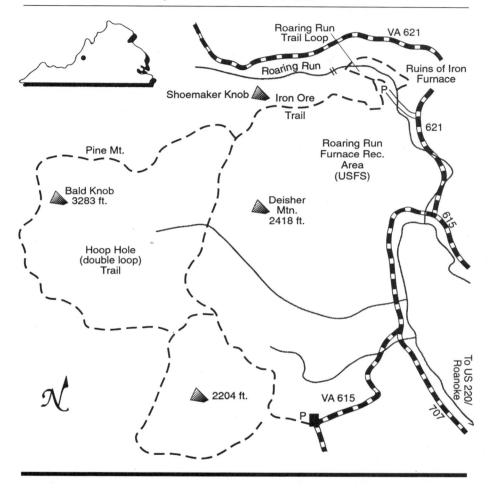

Roaring Run
Trail Loop

VA 621

Roaring Run

Ruins of Iron
Furnace

P

Shoemaker Knob

Iron Ore
Trail

621

Pine Mt.

Roaring Run
Furnace Rec.
Area
(USFS)

Bald Knob
3283 ft.

Deisher
Mtn.
2418 ft.

Hoop Hole
(double loop)
Trail

615

N

2204 ft.

VA 615

To US 220/
Roanoke

707

P

direction you hike, the yellow-blazed, four-mile loop goes up and then descends gorgelike drainages, the most prominent of which is Stony Run on the east side of the loop. Early June is the prime time to see rhododendron blooming on the steep stream banks.

The upper loop, approximately five miles, is a steep, strenuous, and not always easy to follow path that climbs to a point near the crest of Rich Patch Mountain. The trail ascends via Bald Knob and Pine Mountain, ridges from the higher peak. The area, which is rugged and isolated, was once considered for wilderness designation. Experienced hikers will like this hike.

Near the bottom of the loop, a .5-mile side trail reaches the site of an old sawmill, one source of the "hoop poles" that were cut in the area to make barrel staves. Somehow, "hoop pole" became "hoop hole," giving the trail its unusual name. Near the top of the upper loop, there are good views from clifftops.

The yellow-blazed Iron Ore Trail runs between the northeastern-most corner of the upper Hoop Hole loop, and the Roaring Run Trail. From the Roaring Run Trail, the Iron Ore Trail branches left in the picnic area, and climbs on an old road grade, then becomes a rugged foot path on a ridge to its junction with the Hoop Hole Trail. The Iron Ore Trail is 2.4 miles long.

A variety of hikes are possible, including a loop of the upper Hoop Hole Trail starting from the Roaring Run picnic area, a circuit of nine miles. Backpack camping is permitted on the Hoop Hole Trail (and even in the parking lot), but not in the Roaring Run picnic area or on the Roaring Run Trail, both classified as day use areas.

# Douthat State Park

Douthat was one of Virginia's original six state parks. It's rugged mountain setting, isolation, and wealth of facilities make it a perfect base of operation for hikers.

The list of attractions at Douthat State Park is long. With more than forty miles of trails, Douthat's trail mileage exceeds that of any other Virginia state park. Those paths also connect to trails in the George Washington National Forest, and the general vicinity of the park makes it easy to reach many more prime hiking areas. Best of all, Douthat's trails aren't just obligatory state park paths. They reach fine scenic destinations.

Despite being a good day hiking destination, Douthat entices hikers to drop in for a longer stay. Luckily the park's reasonably priced campground, cabins, lodge, and restaurant make that an affordable option.

In fact, few parks welcome hikers with more appropriate accommodations. As one of Virginia's earliest parks, Douthat's facilities were almost exclusively built by the Civilian Conservation Corps. The rustic artistry of those Depression-era craftsmen is an unmistakable presence in the park. Twenty-five log cabins date from the decade between 1933 and 1942 when 600 CCC workers toiled at Douthat. The men also built the restaurant and lodge, the latter a palatially rustic, 3,000-square-foot, six-bedroom cabin.

Today, those accommodations bring the CCC era back for park guests who notice unaltered cabin details such as hand-carved door knobs and hinges, as well as hand-wrought hinges, light fixtures and latches on doors and shutters. Douthat is very nearly a monument to the Civilian Conservation Corps. It was designated as a Registered Historic Landmark in 1986.

Virtually every facility you would expect in a Virginia state park is available here. The only exceptions are bridle trails and horse rentals, bike trails, and motor boating.

The park lies between two massive ridges that reach up to 2,600 and 3,100 feet. Trails throughout this 4,493-acre gem reach scenic overlooks, cascading waterfalls, and towering forests. A fifty-acre lake, at 1,446 feet, shimmers in the valley where the park's facilities are located.

The park visitor center (open Memorial Day weekend through Labor Day), built by the CCC and refurbished in 1988, has exhibits about the CCC's work in the park. There's an environmental education center and interpretive

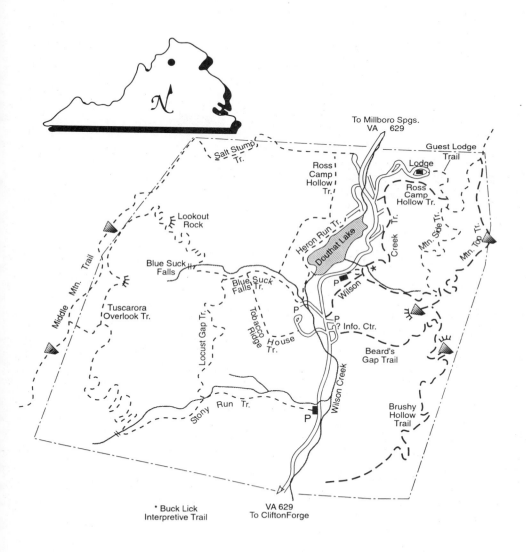

*A typical trailside scene in Virginia's storied forests.*

programs, a lodge, a restaurant, three campgrounds (112 sites, bathhouses, third Saturday in March to the end of October), thirty cabins (through September), and picnic areas (reservations available). Recreational amenities include a swimming beach (bathhouse, concession area), a trout-stocked lake and stream, and boat rentals and boat launch. The lake and Wilson Creek are stocked twice weekly with trout between the third Saturday in March and Labor Day. The park offers a daily trou t fishing program. Backpack camping is not permitted in Douthat State Park.

A $1 parking fee is charged, as are campground fees. Sites may be reserved in advance year-round for an additional fee by phone or mail from Virginia State Parks Reservation Center, P.O. Box 1895, Richmond, Virginia, 23215-1815 (800) 933-7275, 9 a.m.-4 p.m., Monday through Friday, with check, money order, Visa or MC.

The park is located in Bath and Allegheny counties north of Covington, Virginia. Take exit 8 from Interstate 64, and the park office is seven miles north on VA 629. For more park information, contact: Douthat State Park, Route 1, Box 212, Millboro, VA 24460, (540) 862-8100.

# HIKE 14 *BLUE SUCK FALLS/STONY RUN FALLS CIRCUIT*

**General description:** A challenging circuit hike to Douthat State Park's highest elevations atop Middle Mountain. This nine-mile hike climbs and descends past waterfalls, with panoramic views at the higher elevations.

**Elevation gain and loss:** 3,334 feet.

**Trailhead elevation:** 1,333 feet.

**High point:** 3,000 feet.

**Water availability:** Available in season at many of the park's developed facilities. In winter, water is available at the ranger office, open year round, even though the adjacent visitor center is closed in winter.

**Finding the trailhead:** The hike begins at the Stony Run Trail parking area on the west side of the park's main road, VA 629, about a half mile south of the visitor center.

**The hike:** This strenuous circuit hike has it all—deep woods and waterfalls, scenic vistas and ridgetop views. The hike climbs the orange-blazed Stony Run Trail along the stream of the same name. The Locust Gap Trail intersects on the right at about mile 1.5. The trail is pretty gradual all the way to Stony Run Falls, located at about 1,900 feet in elevation, and reached at the 2.5-mile mark.

Middle Mountain steepens significantly above the falls, but the trail switchbacks to minimize the grade. At 4.5 miles, turn right on the yellow-blazed Tuscarora Overlook Trail. In a half mile, reach a two-acre clearing, a perfect picnic spot with a recently "maintained" view that is probably the best in the park. A restored CCC cabin offers rustic shelter.

At about the six mile mark, take a right turn to start the descent on the three-mile Blue Suck Falls Trail. At the 2,560-foot elevation is Lookout Rock, one of this trail's most spectacular overlooks. The trail descends in switchbacks, passes the Pine Tree Trail and crosses the stream below Blue Suck Falls.

The Blue Suck Falls Trail ends, for a nine-mile hike, at the fisherman's parking area near a low water bridge in the group camping area. To avoid following the paved road from the group camping area, on the way down the trail, turn right on the Tobacco House Ridge Trail about .25 mile above the parking area. That path will keep you in the woods for another .8 mile to its exit behind the bathhouse in Campground C. That requires only a .5-mile-walk south to your car on VA 629.

There are other options from the Tuscorora Overlook area. Hikers who go left at the junction between the Blue Suck Falls and Tuscorora Overlook trails will shortly reach the white-blazed Middle Mountain Trail along the ridgetop. Going south on this trail, hikers will reach a wooded summit at 3,187 feet after .1 mile. This is the highest elevation in the area easily reachable by trail.

Going north, hikers can lengthen the loop described above by descending the Salt Stump Trail to a trailhead in Campground B, for a hike of 10.5 miles (requires a second car). Hikers using that route could also join Backway Hollow Trail near Campground B and hike on the Huff's, Blue Suck Falls, and Tobacco House Ridge trails to the area of the visitor center for a more than thirteen-mile hike, not including the .5-mile roadside walk to the Stony Run Trail parking area.

Remember, you needn't tackle a nine-mile hike to see the waterfalls. Round trip hikes to either cascade, omitting the trip to the summit, are about five miles.

# HIKE 15 MOUNTAIN TOP AND MOUNTAIN SIDE TRAIL CIRCUIT

**General description:** A moderate 4.3-mile hike to views from Beards Mountain in Douthat State Park.
**Elevation gain and loss:** 1,730 feet.
**Trailhead elevation:** 1,755 feet.
**High point:** 2,620 feet.
**Water availability:** Available in season at many of the park's developed facilities. In winter, water is available at the park's ranger office, open year round, even though the adjacent visitor center is closed.
**Finding the trailhead:** The hike starts on the Guest Lodge Trail, which begins at the park lodge, a CCC-built facility reached by a side road to the cabin area.

**The hike:** This nearly 4.5-mile circuit hike climbs gradually to mountaintop views looking down on the state park and across the valley to Middle Mountain.

Starting on the Guest Lodge Trail, the hike passes the Ross Camp Hollow Trail, entering from the right. Not far beyond, take the next left, on the Mountain Top Trail, about .5 mile from the lodge.

The Mountain Top Trail ascends northeast, rounding the ridges on the way to a gap atop Beards Mountain. Go right, south along the ridge, passing over the 2,620-foot point of Beards Mountain, and descending to a junction with the Mountain Side Trail, just under three miles from the lodge.

Circuit hikers will want to turn right and head back to the lodge, but good views are not far away, reached by continuing south on the Mountain Top Trail. Just .1 mile further, and beyond a junction to the right with the Buck Lick Trail, a spur trail reaches an overlook, at 2,110 feet. This area is the least visited in the park, and trails here are less intensively maintained than those to Blue Suck Falls and other popular destinations. The footing may be rugged in spots, and the path may be less than two feet wide.

To reach views further south, take the Brushy Hollow Trail that drops down a little less than 200 feet in elevation into Beard's Gap. The trail then climbs to another fine overlook at 2,360 feet, just under one mile (roundtrip) from the junction of the Mountain Top and Mountain Side trails.

Back at the Mountain Top and Mountain Side trail junction, turn north and descend on the Mountain Side Trail to the Guest Lodge Trail at about 4.3 miles. The Guest Lodge Trail returns you to your car in less than five miles, minus any additional distance to optional viewpoints.

Alternatives include dropping into the valley on the Buck Hollow Trail, and then reaching the lodge via the Wilson Creek, Ross Camp Hollow, and Guest Lodge trails, a circuit of about 6.5 miles. In the winter, the road to the Guest Lodge Trail may be gated. If it is, park in the lot beside State Route 629, and take the Ross Camp Trail that starts near cabin 12.

# HIKE 16 *DOUTHAT STATE PARK NATURE WALKS*

**General description:** The Heron Run Trail, .8 mile one way, is an easy lakeshore path through tall hemlocks. The Buck Lick Interpretive Trail, a less than .5-mile loop, is keyed to educational signs.

**Elevation gain and loss:** Negligible.

**Trailhead elevation:** 1,450-1,550 feet.

**Water availability:** Available in season at many places in the park's developed facilities. In winter, water is available at the park office.

**Finding the trailheads:** The Heron Run Trail begins in the lakeside loop of Campground A in the park. The Buck Lick Interpretive Trail begins in a parking area on the right near the public phone at the entrance to the lakeside concession area.

**The hikes:** The Heron Run Trail is the park's best easy trail. The Buck Lick Trail is the park's educational nature loop and another legacy from the Civilian Conservation Corps.

The Heron Run Trail has been opened in recent years and is a level, nicely benched trail that borders fifty-acre Douthat Lake. Hikers can wander the coves along the lakeshore for .8 mile through tall timber, then retrace their steps. The lake's dam and outlet stream prevent a loop hike, so the entire hike is about 1.5 miles.

The Buck Lick Trail circles back to its starting point in .3 mile. Along the way, interpretive signs point out key elements of the local forest, including tree species like white oak and tulip poplar. Among the trail's impressive evergreens are white pine, hemlock, and rhododendron.

*A fern-filled forest yields to a mountain meadow in the George Washington National Forest.*

# Ramseys Draft Wilderness

# HIKE 17 *RAMSEYS DRAFT TRAIL*

**General description:** Moderate to strenuous trails offer day hiking and backpacking in and around a 6,519-acre wilderness, about twenty miles west of Staunton. The Ramseys Draft is known for what may be Virginia's most impressive virgin hemlock forest.
**Elevation gain and loss:** 4,044 feet.
**Trailhead elevation:** 2,260 feet.
**High point:** 4,282 feet.
**Water availability:** Available in season at Mountain House Picnic Area, U.S. Forest Service developed picnic area at trailhead. Also, trail parallels major stream from wilderness drainage.
**Finding the trailhead:** Trail starts at U.S. Forest Service Mountain House Picnic Area on US 250, fifteen miles west of Churchville, Virginia.

**The hike:** The Ramseys Draft Trail follows the cold and rushing stream, the Ramseys Draft. An entire network of trails, a few of them new, tie into that central trail to create a fine series of circuit hikes.

Unfortunately, the Ramseys Draft Trail was washed out in many places by a major flood in 1985. That ended the easy, road-width access hikers had to the towering hemlocks that lined the trails and grew in trailless coves between the peaks. Even before the flood, hikers on the trail had to ford the stream more than ten times, so the Ramseys Draft Trail had its element of effort even then.

Today, some sections of the trail are much as they were before the flood. Others are blocked every few yards with debris that has been purposely left by the forest service. The idea, bolstered by Virginia's well-organized citizen preservationists, was to leave the wilderness as nature left it, and let hikers experience it on those terms. That has certainly cut down on the ease with which hikers reach the heart of this scenic area. Land managers and wilderness purists see benefits to that; some struggling hikers may not.

The trails described here do not have consistent blazing or official blaze colors. Signs are few, and the official forest service map of the Ramseys Draft Wilderness has a rather major error on it, which has been corrected on the map included in this book. This trail description will alert you to that error.

Despite the forest service interest in keeping the trails primitive, they say that if informal trails become established around obstacles left by the flood, and they begin to create resource damage, some clearing may be authorized to focus use in areas that can better absorb the impact.

To compensate, the trails that flank "the Draft" have been upgraded, and two paths added that create a major loop around the wilderness. That doesn't make it any easier to hike up and down the stream, but at least the enhanced circuit hike that loops the wilderness enables hikers to bite the bullet and hike downhill on the Ramseys Draft Trail as the exit leg of a day hike or backpacking trip. Despite the debris, serious hikers and backpackers will want to consider seeing the Draft.

# HIKES 17 & 18 *RAMSEYS DRAFT TRAIL & SHENANDOAH MOUNTAIN TRAIL*

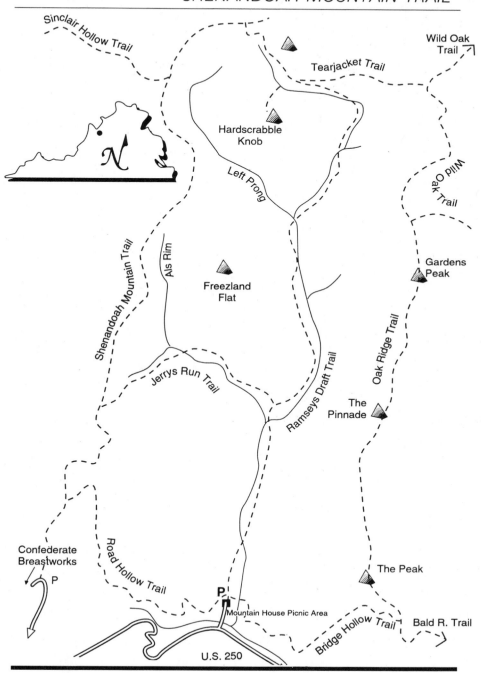

Sinclair Hollow Trail

Wild Oak Trail

Tearjacket Trail

Hardscrabble Knob

Left Prong

Wild Oak Trail

Shenandoah Mountain Trail

Als Rim

Freezland Flat

Gardens Peak

Jerrys Run Trail

Ramseys Draft Trail

Oak Ridge Trail

The Pinnade

Confederate Breastworks

P

Road Hollow Trail

P

Mountain House Picnic Area

The Peak

U.S. 250

Bridge Hollow Trail

Bald R. Trail

Before the flood, hikers chose to hike up and down the stream, or use the more westerly Shenandoah Mountain Trail on the way in or out. That option always required bushwhacking back to your car in the valley, or on the ridge. The same inconvenient situation faced hikers who focused on the ridge to the east of the Ramseys Draft Trail, the Bald Ridge Trail. All three of those paths connected at the northern end of the draft, so the only thing missing were parking area connections on the southern end between the Draft Trail and the ridgetop trails to the east and west.

Now those connectors exist. Both begin from the Ramseys Draft Trail parking area, about 100 yards from US 250 on the road into the Mountain House Picnic Area.

The Road Hollow Trail, just finished in 1992, heads west from the parking area (2,260 feet) climbing gradually outside the wilderness through Road Hollow to a junction with the Shenandoah Mountain Trail (approximately 2,960 feet) in two miles. (See **Shenandoah Mountain Trail** for details on that hike past the Jerry's Run Trail to the vicinity of Hardscrabble Knob.)

The Bridge Hollow Trail, opened in 1989, heads east from the parking area outside the wilderness and climbs in two miles to the Bald Ridge Trail, at approximately 3,400 feet. Having gained the top of Bald Ridge, hikers can head north on the Bald Ridge Trail to create a loop of the Ramseys Draft.

Going south, the Bald Ridge Trail winds off the ridge to its own trailhead at the U.S. Forest Service's Braley Pond Picnic Area, after about four miles. That trailhead is reached from the east by turning right from US 250 onto VA Route 715 ten miles west of Churchville, approximately .5 mile before West Augusta, a small community at the junction with VA Route 629. In less than .5 mile on VA 715, Forest Development Road 349.1 heads left one mile to Braley Pond. Find the Braley Pond Loop Trail in the picnic area and take it .5 mile to the upper end of the pond, and the trail junction.

On the Bald Ridge Trail, the route north ranges between 3,600 and just under 4,000 feet, crossing summits such as The Peak, 3,674 feet; The Pinnacle, 3,841 feet; and Gordon's Peak, 3,915 feet.

In a gap at four miles (six miles from the Ramseys Draft parking area), the Wild Oak Trail (the old Dividing Ridge Trail) comes in from the right and takes the place of the Bald Ridge Trail.

The Wild Oak National Recreation Trail is a 25.6-mile loop hike that coincides with the circuit around Ramseys Draft for only a short distance. A small part of this trail is a road (not in the vicinity of Ramseys Draft) that is open to vehicles from October through December. Nevertheless, the Wild Oak Trail is a nice, and rugged, three-day backpacking loop that avoids the more popular Ramseys Draft area, while touching it for a short distance. Write to the forest service's Dry River Ranger District to receive a free pamphlet describing the trail.

To start the Draft loop from the Wild Oak Trail, take the same route as described for the Bald Ridge Trail, but stay on VA Route 715, which becomes FDR 96, and reaches the trailhead on the left about four miles from US 250. It is approximately 2.1 miles from the trailhead on FDR 96 to the Bald Ridge Trail.

Hikers starting from the Ramseys Draft parking area will be on the White Oak Trail for 1.6 miles north. That section of trail crosses Big Bald Knob, about 4,100 feet. Beyond Big Bald Knob, the Wild Oak Trail swings east at 7.6 miles from the Ramseys Draft Parking Area, and Ramseys Draft hikers

*The bald summit of trailless Freezland Flat, in the Ramseys Draft Wilderness.*

will go left on the Tearjacket Trail (the old Springhouse Ridge Trail) towards Tearjacket Knob, the area's second highest peak, at 4,229 feet.

From the Tearjacket/Wild Oak junction, the Wild Oak Trail descends east to Camp Todd, another access point. Follow the above directions for the Bald Ridge Trail, continue two miles past the first Wild Oak trailhead to a left turn on FDR 95. A large Camp Todd sign on the left in three miles indicates the start of the trail.

The Tearjacket Trail skirts the very head of the Draft, then dips into the Draft and joins the Ramsey's Draft Trail 8.8 miles from the Mountain House Picnic Area parking. BE AWARE that the U.S. Forest Service map (1987) of the Ramseys Draft does not show this junction. The map mistakenly shows the Tearjacket Trail staying above the Draft Trail, crossing the summit of Tearjacket Knob and joining the Shenandoah Mountain Trail. To correct your map, drop the Tearjacket Trail into the Draft Trail at Hiner Spring.

After entering the Ramseys Draft Trail from the Tearjacket Trail, Hiner Spring is about fifty yards ahead. A side trail goes left at nine miles to Hardscrabble Knob, and the Shenandoah Mountain Trail is reached at 9.8 miles.

Following the Shenandoah Mountain Trail to the right offers another option for easy access to this area. The trail ends at FSR 95 in three miles, passing scenic Puffenbarger Meadows on the way. That trailhead is reached using the same route as described for the Bald Ridge Trail. Follow that route to a left turn from FSR 96 onto FSR 95. The trailhead is 4.5 miles past Camp Todd.

Continuing the loop of the wilderness with a left on the Shenandoah Mountain Trail, the Ramseys Draft parking area is another 7.5 miles, via the Road Hollow Trail, for a total circuit of just over seventeen miles.

The most gradual way to hike the loop around the Ramseys Draft is to reverse the directions above. In that direction, the hike yields these mileages: Shenandoah Mountain Trail via Road Hollow Trail, two miles; Jerry's Run Trail, about three miles; Ramseys Draft Trail, about 7.5 miles; junction of Tearjacket Trail, about 8.5 miles; and Wild Oak Trail, 9.7 miles; junction of Wild Oak Trail and Bald Ridge Trail, 11.3 miles; junction of Bald Ridge and Bridge Hollow Trail, 15.3; and the Ramseys Draft Trail parking at the Mountain House Picnic Area, just over seventeen miles.

The Ramseys Draft Trail bisects the two ridge routes, rising gradually from 2,260 feet to 3,800 feet at the Shenandoah Mountain Trail. The trail follows the main stream, while the Jerry's Run Trail branches left up Jerry's Run at 1.6 miles. The trailless Left Prong of the Ramseys Draft goes left at 3.5 miles, and the Ramseys Draft Trail follows the Right Prong.

Between the two prongs of the stream is Hardscrabble Knob, highest peak in the wilderness at 4,282 feet, an old firetower site. The Ramseys Draft Trail passes a junction with the Tearjacket Trail at about 5.5 miles, and Hiner Spring is on the left fifty yards beyond. A side trail at 5.6 miles, also to the left, reaches the summit of Hardscrabble Knob in less than .5 mile. The Ramseys Draft Trail intersects the Shenandoah Mountain Trail at 6.5 miles.

There are numerous circuit hiking options. The least ambitious for day hikers climbs Road Hollow to the Shenandoah Mountain Trail, heads north and makes a descent through Jerry's Run, returning downhill on the Ramseys Draft Trail for 1.5 mile. Energetic day hikes and overnight trips could circle the entire area, or loop half the wilderness using either ridge.

The heart of this wilderness is best appreciated by avoiding the trails. Experienced hikers should consider trailless hiking. The most obvious bushwhack routes at times display evidence of occasional use. Off-trail hikers and especially campers should use care not to damage the fragile beauty of the Ramseys Draft. The forest service requests "no-trace" camping in the wilderness. Luckily, substantial portions of the wilderness are made up of open forest, easily navigated with little damage to vegetation.

It is quite easy to start any one of the circuit hikes above, and make it substantially shorter by dropping into one of the untrailed drainages that lead to Ramseys Draft. When you consider the primitive trail maintenance policy being followed here, especially along the Ramseys Draft Trail, you might just as well opt for no trail at all.

Among the most popular trailless routes is the Left Prong, the heart of the forest service "natural area" that was established in 1935 to preserve the extensive groves of virgin timber. Some of these inspiring trees are over 300 years old.

Trailless options also include the oddly spelled destination, Freezland Flat (4,050 feet), a no doubt bitterly cold summit in a winter storm. The peak is topped by a natural meadow, and hemmed-in by a fern carpeted hardwood forest.

# HIKE 18 *SHENANDOAH MOUNTAIN TRAIL*

**General description:** An easy out (7.1 miles) and back (14.2 miles) hike, perfect for cross-country skiing, and a nice addition to a hike in the Ramseys Draft Wilderness Area.

**Elevation gain and loss:** Approximately 1,200 feet.

**Trailhead elevation:** Approximately 3,000 feet.

**High point:** 3,600 feet.

**Water availability:** Water is available in season two miles east of the trailhead on US 250 at Mountain House Picnic Area.

**Finding the trailhead:** The trail begins atop Shenandoah Mountain, seventeen miles west of Churchville, Virginia on US 250, two miles west of the U.S. Forest Service's Mountain House Picnic Area.

**The hike:** Shenandoah Mountain isn't a spectacular hike, in the sense of alpine grandeur. But it is a very scenic, gradual, and lengthy ridgetop ramble with occasional views, mostly to the west toward West Virginia.

The elevation, 3,000 to 3,500 feet, is high enough to support northern tree species such as beech, birch, and maple, with hemlocks and even spruce scattered around. That forest explodes into autumn beauty, making this a great fall hike. And with the snowy wilds of West Virginia within sight, Shenandoah Mountain receives enough snow to offer fine cross-country skiing. This trail wouldn't be so skiable if it wasn't gradual. For mile after mile, the Shenandoah Mountain Trail easily undulates on long grades. This also makes it the perfect place to ski, carry a heavy pack, or hike with children or the elderly.

The trail follows the western edge of the Ramseys Draft Wilderness, a pocket of virgin forest unlike any other in the state. The Shenandoah Mountain Trail connects with three trails that explore the Draft, making it an integral part of the wilderness trail system.

The trail starts where US 250 crosses the ridge of Shenandoah Mountain at a U.S. Forest Service interpretive site called the Confederate Breastworks. From the trailhead, the Shenandoah Mountain Trail is combined with the short path that loops through the Civil War observation post.

At .3 mile, the blue-blazed main trail continues beyond the shorter loop trail, and at about 1.5 mile, the relatively new Road Hollow Trail comes in from the right. This is one of two new trails in the area, just south of the Ramseys Draft Wilderness, that are intended to create new loop hiking opportunities that encircle the wilderness. That is intended to compensate for the fact that the trail along the Ramseys Draft stream was extensively washed out by a flood in 1985 and will not be restored to its previous high standard.

Luckily, this creates another access point for the Shenandoah Mountain Trail. Using the Road Hollow Trail, set for finalization in 1992, hikers can start at the Ramseys Draft parking area in the valley, and with a two mile hike, join the Shenandoah Mountain Trail.

*A lone backpacker winds through explosive fall foliage on the gradual Shenandoah Mountain Trail.*

At 2.4 miles on the Shenandoah Mountain Trail, the Jerry's Run Trail branches right into Ramsey's Draft. (That creates a nice smaller loop for hikers using the Road Hollow Trail and returning down the Ramseys Draft Trail to their car in the valley.) Water is available .3 mile down the Jerry's Run Trail at a spring that used to serve the Sexton Shelter. The Sexton Shelter was a Potomac Appalachian Trail Club cabin that was removed after the area became a federal wilderness, a designation that prohibits permanent manmade structures.

The Sinclair Hollow Trail descends left at 6.6 miles (1.8 miles to Shaw's Fork Road). At 7.1 miles, the Ramsey's Draft Trail intersects from the right, after having followed a tumbling stream through the wilderness for 6.5 miles from the Ramsey's Draft main parking area.

Backpackers might focus on the area of the Shenandoah Mountain/Ramseys Draft Trail junction, as campsites are plentiful. Hiner Spring is 1.1 miles down the Ramsey's Draft Trail on the right, and on the way, a side trail climbs to Hardscrabble Knob, former site of a fire tower and the area's highest peak at 4,282 feet.

Because the Shenandoah Mountain Trail winds in and out of the wilderness, forest service trail maintainers have adopted a more rustic trail maintenance philosophy. They say public sentiment seems to support less maintenance, which means the once widely pruned Shenandoah Mountain Trail has grown-in and in some places the nicely benched treadway is growing up with brushy vegetation.

That is bad news for cross-country skiers, because all the Shenandoah Mountain Trail needs to be a great Nordic ski trail is for the brush to be trimmed back far enough to permit smooth travel. Luckily, the forest service says increased maintenance is planned for 1992. Even if the past width of the trail is not restored, certainly a cleared path is not out of place on a trail that is in fact outside the wilderness in many places. Skiers might make that sentiment known to the forest service if they find the trail unsuitable for skiing.

# The Blue Ridge Parkway

This 469-mile motor trail (free) winds from the Skyline Drive (fee) in Shenandoah National Park, at Interstate 64, south through the George Washington and Jefferson national forests into North Carolina. It ends at Great Smoky Mountains National Park.

Of that total, 217 miles lie in Virginia, most of that following a ridgetop route. Dozens of overlooks are scattered along the way. Trails begin at many of them. Since the motor experience is primary on this road, rated one of America's most scenic, the trails are only a sidelight. Few are very long, most are defined as "leg-stretchers"—options for the cramped motorist more than avenues of exploration for serious trail enthusiasts.

Nevertheless, some great hiking is available on the parkway. There are short trails that are worth a long drive, and longer trails that make nice day hikes. Backpacking is only permitted on one Blue Ridge Parkway trail system, but some tie-in to larger trail networks, many of those in nearby national forests.

Not all parkway trails are covered here; just a handful of those that reflect the Parkway's broad spectrum of trail experiences. Trails described in this book include the Humpback Rocks Trail (mileposts 5 to 9), the Sharp Top, Harkening Hill and other trails at Peaks of Otter (mileposts 84 to 87), and trails to Saint Mary's Wilderness (milepost 22).

Other noteworthy paths are scattered along the length of the Parkway. At the low point on the road (649 feet at milepost 63), where the Parkway crosses the James River, the Trail of Trees begins. This interpretive trail,

*Humpback Rocks as seen from the Blue Ridge Parkway.* Virginia Division of Tourism photo.

which extends less than .5 mile, provides nice views of the James and its impressive cleavage of the Blue Ridge. Across the river, the James River Face Wilderness (see entry) descends in a tangled plummet to the river. Also nearby is the James River Trail that leads to riverside views and canal locks used in the last century when the Kanawha Canal was a vital trade link from Richmond to the west.

At milepost 78, the Apple Orchard Falls Trail leaves Sunset Field Overlook for a scenic, 1.2-mile downhill hike to the falls. The climb back to the overlook creates a 2.4 mile round trip that is strenuous but rewarding. At milepost 154, the three-mile Smart View Loop Trail displays a diversity of trail settings and good views in the vicinity of the Smart View Picnic Area.

At milepost 167, the Rock Castle Gorge National Recreation Trail descends into a spectacular gorge included in the Rocky Knob Recreation Area, one of many places where the Blue Ridge Parkway "bulges" out beyond its normal .5-mile strip of land to encompass expanded recreational options. Rock Castle Gorge is a strenuous, rugged hike that can be anywhere from six to more than ten miles when combined with other trails.

The Gorge Trail is one of only two places on the Blue Ridge Parkway property where backpack camping is permitted. The other is Doughton Park's Basin Cove area in North Carolina. Campers must have a free camping permit acquired at the visitor center. Be aware also that because backpack camping is restricted, fires are never permitted on parkway trails. Also, dogs must always be leashed on parkway paths.

Virginia's seven developed parkway recreation areas combine to offer four campgrounds (Otter Creek, Peaks of Otter, Roanoke Mountain, and Rocky Knob), four picnic areas (Humpback Rocks, Peaks of Otter, Smart View, and Rocky Knob), four visitor centers (Humpback Rocks, James River, Peaks of Otter, and Rocky Knob), four restaurants (Whetstone Ridge, Otter Creek, Peaks of Otter, and Mabry Mill), gas stations, and lodging at Peaks of Otter and Rocky Knob.

Attractions at these recreation areas range from a variety of trails to restored mountaineer cabins and an impressive grist mill at Mabry Mill. Developed parkway facilities are generally open from May to October, with few exceptions, such as the year-round lodging at Peaks of Otter Lodge.

Access to the parkway in winter is possible at many plowed road crossings,but snow can prompt the closure of the road, ending efforts to enjoy a winter hike on the Blue Ridge Parkway. Without snow, all of the road remains open through the winter. With snow on the ground, and the roads gated, cross-country skiers are permitted to use the road as a trail. Perhaps the best place to focus winter use, with snow on the ground, is Peaks of Otter. Virginia Route 43 crosses the parkway there, and becomes part of the road for a distance, so public transportation requires that it be plowed. That gives access to a number of trails, plus developed winter car camping and the Peaks of Otter Lodge—a fine lodging and dining destination year-round (Peaks of Otter Lodge, Box 489, Bedford, VA 24523, (540) 586-1081 or (800) 542-5927.

Individual maps are available for each of the parkway's developed recreation areas and can be picked up at visitor centers and ranger stations. For general information, and a nice color map of the park, write: **Blue Ridge Parkway, 400 BB&T Building, Asheville, NC 28801; 704-298-0398.**

# HIKE 19
## JAMES RIVER FACE/THUNDER RIDGE WILDERNESSES AND TRAILS

**General description:** Virginia's first wilderness area, designated in 1975, the 9,000-acre James River Face is a rugged and scenic area that clings to the cliffs where the mighty James River breaks through the Blue Ridge. Thunder Ridge, one of Virginia's "newest" wilderness areas, is about 2,500 acres just south of the James River Face. There are few easy hikes in this area. Most are strenuous and loop hikes are few.

**Elevation gain and loss:** Approximately 4,846 feet between lowest Appalachian Trailhead and Highcock Knob.

**Trailhead elevation:** Approximately 660 feet near James River.

**High point:** Approximately 3,073 feet at Highcock Knob.

**Water availability:** Water is available in season north of the James River Face at the Blue Ridge Parkway's Otter Creek Recreation Area (milepost 61) and the James River Visitor Center (milepost 63). Water is found at various springs, mentioned under trail descriptions, but many trails are dry. For day hikes, the most convenient option may be to bring water with you.

**Finding the trailheads:** The James River Face is located south of the James River and is flanked on the east by the Blue Ridge Parkway between mileposts 67 and 71. Thunder Ridge Wilderness lies just south of James River Face, between Blue Ridge Parkway mileposts 71 and 76.5.

Many trailheads are available along this part of the Blue Ridge Parkway. Other trailheads will be described under their entries. To reach the Parkway at the James River, from the west, take I-81 exits 49 or 50, approximately eight and twelve miles respectively to Glasgow. There take U.S. 501 nine miles to the parkway.

From the east, exit U.S. 29 or U.S. 460 at Lynchburg and take U.S. 501 west approximately twenty miles to the Blue Ridge Parkway.

**The hike:** Together, the James River Face and Thunder Ridge comprise an 11,500-acre wilderness tract that rises from the deceptive calm of the mighty James River to the lofty altitude of Highcock Knob and the Blue Ridge Parkway.

Much of the area was logged earlier in the century, and many of the trails follow road grades that were no doubt part of that process. Nevertheless, the rugged, precipitous faces that plummet toward the James likely possess significant parcels of timber that escaped early loggers. But trees here rarely tower to stereotypically primeval proportions. The thin, rocky soils that cover most of the area support scrubby communities of Virginia pine, chestnut oak, and heath type undergrowth, such as mountain laurel.

The rocky character of the area breaks out of the vegetation at the Devils Marbleyard, an eight-acre slope of quartzite boulders located on the Belfast Trail.

The deeper coves are home to the hemlocks and white pines, but few trails venture there. This is an area of radiating ridgetop trails that make loop hiking difficult. End to end, actually car-to-car hikes are the best way to see the area.

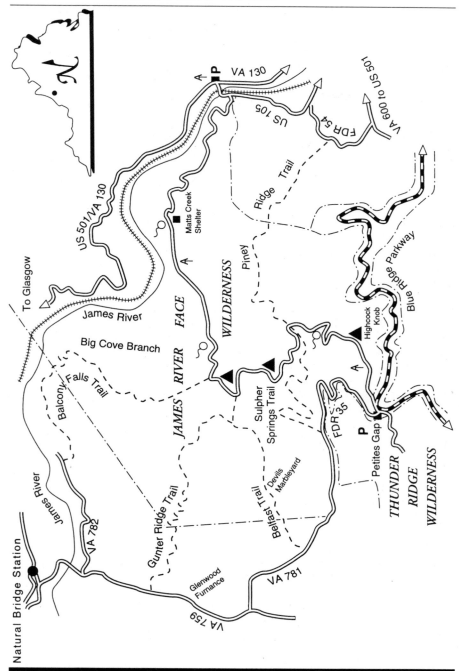

VA 130

US 105

FDR 54

VA 600 to US 501

US 501/VA 130

To Glasgow

James River

Matts Creek Shelter

Ridge Trail

Piney

WILDERNESS

JAMES RIVER FACE

Big Cove Branch

Balcony Falls Trail

Blue Ridge Parkway

Highcock Knob

Sulpher Springs Trail

FDR 35

Petites Gap

P

THUNDER RIDGE WILDERNESS

James River

VA 782

Gunter Ridge Trail

Belfast Trail

Devils Marbleyard

Natural Bridge Station

Glenwood Furnance

VA 781

VA 759

For that reason, individual trails will be covered separately, and hiking suggestions will be discussed under a later "options" entry. Given the difficulty of arranging those kinds of hikes, and the area's popularity, be sure to choose an "off-season" or midweek time to hike on popular routes like the A.T.

The Thunder Ridge Wilderness is essentially just the sloping western side of the Blue Ridge below the parkway, though that description doesn't do justice to the unique plants that grow there. In general, the area is steep and scrubby enough to discourage bushwhack hiking, at least the casual kind. But for the serious wilderness purist, the trailless James River Face is a wealth of hard to reach places that offer pristine, primeval scenery and total solitude.

## The Appalachian Trail

The A.T. is best hiked south to north to minimize the nearly 2,500-foot climb hikers face going north to south. The white-blazed trail begins its 10.5-mile traverse of the James River Face section in Petites Gap at milepost 71 on the Blue Ridge Parkway (2,369 feet). Forest Service road 35 leaves the parkway there, and descends to State Route 781 and a few other trailheads to be covered later under circuit hikes.

The A.T. departs the gap climbing steeply through stinging trailside vegetation to Highcock Knob, a wooded, 3,073-foot summit at 1.2 miles. The trail then plummets very steeply off the peak, levels off, and arrives at the former site of Marble Spring Shelter about a mile from the summit and just over two miles from the road. The shelter site is now a camping area, with a nice spring down the side trail to the left.

At about 2.7 miles, the Sulphur Spring Trail, an old road grade, crosses the A.T. Left, it descends to State Route 781/FDR 35 and is part of a circuit hike covered later. To the right, the trail soon reaches the Piney Ridge Trail, also a circuit hike option.

For the next few miles the A.T. undulates along the main ridge, skirting the summits on its way to a junction with the Belfast Trail at about 4.5 miles. This trail to the left, and the Gunter Ridge Trail that branches from it, also lead to State Route 781/FDR 35 and are part of a circuit hike described later.

The A.T. turns sharp right at the junction, and .5 mile later, about five miles from the parking area, reaches the north side of the ridge. The Balcony Falls Trail drops left. Here the A.T. begins a descent from 2,600 feet to approximately 660 feet near the James River. Between the ridgetop and Matt's Creek Shelter, at about 7.5 miles, the A.T. offers great views of the James and glimpses of the area's wildest scenery.

Unlike the now removed Marble Spring lean-to, Matt's Creek Shelter is likely to stay, despite being located in a Wilderness area. The local A.T. club has built an impressive new bridge across the gorge-like stream by the shelter. A spring is nearby.

The trail climbs again, more than 500 vertical feet, then descends to become a road grade at about nine miles. The trail reaches U.S. 501 at about 10.3 miles.

One of the easiest hikes in the James River Face Wilderness is an out and back day hike on the A.T. from U.S. 501. Hikers could turn back after having lunch at the shelter, or climb to views of the river gap. Those options create five to ten mile round-trips. To reach this trailhead, go west approximately three miles from the U.S. 501 junction with the Blue Ridge Parkway.

## Belfast Trail

The Belfast Trail leads hikers to one of the wilderness area's most interesting natural features, the Devils Marbleyard. It also facilitates the best circuit hike in the James River Face Wilderness. The Belfast Trail climbs from State Route 781, about 1,010 feet, to the Appalachian Trail, at about 2,660 feet.

The trail crosses the East Fork of Elk Creek on a footbridge, passes an old Boy Scout camp, and then climbs a gradually tightening drainage to the Devils Marbleyard. The open boulderfield provides great views of the Arnold Valley and Thunder Ridge Wilderness Area.

After the steep stretch past the Marbleyard, the trail becomes more gradual and joins the A.T. at 2.8 miles after 2.2 miles in the wilderness.

To reach the trail, exit I-81 as described above, and reach the town of Natural Bridge Station, before Glasgow, on VA 130. Turn south on State Route 759 for a little more than three miles, and turn left on State Route 781. The trailhead is about 1.3 miles. The trail has limited roadside parking, but additional space is on the left nearby.

## Sulphur Spring Trail

This trail provides horse and hiker access to the heart of the Wilderness area. For much of the trail's 6.6 miles, it runs the ridgetop in close proximity to the Appalachian Trail. Hikers can avoid it there, but the lower section from State Route 781/FDR 35 to the A.T. permits one of the area's best circuit hikes when used in conjunction with the Belfast Trail.

The trail climbs via a roadgrade from FSR 35, at about 1,451 feet, past Sulphur Spring to the Appalachian Trail in 2.8 miles, at about 2,460 feet. The trail continues, and hikers may prefer the A.T., but the roadgrade route is there if desired.

To reach the trailhead, follow the directions above for the Belfast Trail, and go .1 mile beyond that trail to the end of the pavement on State Route 781. Half a mile further, the road becomes FDR 35, and the trailhead is reached at 3.2 miles from the turn onto State Route 781.

## Piney Ridge Trail

Just east of the Appalachian Trail via the Sulphur Spring Trail, the strenuous Piney Ridge Trail drops to FDR 54 in 3.5 miles. The trail descends from approximately 2,450 feet to 900 feet on FDR 54.

To reach Piney Ridge Trail, take directions to the A.T. near the James River, and then go south on U.S. 501 to a right turn onto FDR 54. The trailhead is about .5 mile on the right.

## Gunter Ridge Trail

This strenuous trail drops from the Belfast Trail at about 2,500 feet, from .4 mile west of the A.T., to State Route 759 at approximately 800 feet. To reach the trail, exit I-81 as described above, and reach the town of Natural Bridge Station, before Glasgow, on VA 130. Take VA 130 south, then turn south on State Route 759 to the trail, approximately 1.5 miles.

## Balcony Falls Trail

This trail, for the most part an old roadgrade, departs the Appalachian Trail at about five miles from Petites Gap, at an elevation of 2,600 feet. The road

*The densely forested slopes of the James River Face Wilderness plummet into the rapids.*

grade becomes a trail just over a mile from the A.T. The ridgetop views of the James River are superb. On the trail's 5.5-mile descent to State Route 782, the forest shifts from a piney woods to Appalachian hardwoods.

To reach the trail, exit I-81 as described above, and reach the town of Natural Bridge Station, before Glasgow, on VA 130. Turn south on State Route 759 and immediately after crossing the James River, turn left on State Route 782. Trailhead is about 1.8 miles on the right.

## Hiking Options

The out-and-back options are numerous, but the hiker's desire to circuit hike through the James River Face will be largely frustrated. There are possibilities though, and the above trail entries should permit you to calculate the mileage of your own preferred route.

Perhaps the best circuit is the climb up the Belfast Trail, traverse of the A.T. and descent of the Sulphur Spring Trail for an approximately 7.4-mile hike. Hikers should then descend the unpaved forest road for a mile to their vehicles. That's about as close as you can come to a circuit hike in the Face.

Another similar climb, up the A.T., and a descent of the Piney Ridge Trail, like a circuit up and down the Gunter Ridge and Balcony Falls trails, will probably require two cars. Luckily, these trailheads on both sides of the wilderness are close enough together that little time will be lost shuttling cars great distances.

# HIKE 20 *HENRY LANUM TRAIL*

*(formerly Pompey and Mt. Pleasant Loop Trail)*

**General description:** An easy to moderate, five-mile loop trail in the central Blue Ridge with spectacular views on Mt. Pleasant. The loop is adjacent to the Old Hotel/Appalachian Trail circuit and together they offer highly recommended day and overnight hiking options.

**Elevation gain and loss:** Approximately 1,194 feet.

**Trailhead elevation:** 3,435 feet.

**High point:** 4,032 feet.

**Water availability:** Three springs are located on the trail, two at about the three-mile mark.

**Finding the trailhead:** The trail starts at a major trailhead parking area, just under five miles from U.S. 60 via State Routes 634 and 755, and FDRs 48 and 51. Reach the trailhead by taking U.S. 60 west from Amherst (via U.S. 29 about fifteen miles north of Lynchburg, and about forty-five miles south of exit 22 on I-64 near Charlottesville). From U.S. 60, turn right onto State Route 634 at about 18.3 miles from Amherst. Turn right onto State Route 755, and continue on FDR 48 when state maintenance ends. Reach Hog Camp Gap, the Appalachian Trail crossing, and proceed the last .5 mile to the trailhead on FDR 51.

From January to March, a gate blocks the road at Hog Camp Gap, requiring hikers to walk to the parking area.

**The hike:** The Henry Lanum Trail, formerly called the Pompey and Mt. Pleasant Loop Trail, embodies an interesting quandary for hikers. There are Virginia hiking destinations that are far better-known and more spectacular than this modest five-mile loop. The same can be said for the adjoining Old Hotel Trail circuit. Eventually though, there comes a time when you've hiked the more famous trails, or just seen as many other people as you care too. Then you consider "other" trails. Among those are the hikes that managing agencies create, or encourage, not necessarily to reach a park's best scenery, but to "expand recreational opportunities."

Actually, the Lanum Trail, and the Old Hotel/Appalachian Trail circuit beside it, probably fall into that "give hikers somewhere else to go" category. In this case, that's fine, because both loops are quite spectacular in spots. But most importantly, both offer solitude, a scarce commodity on some of the more popular paths. That situation would please Henry Lanum, the avid hiker who designed this loop, and in partnership with the forest service, saw that it was opened for public use. Lanum, who recently died, was the long-time trail supervisor for the Natural Bridge Appalachian Trail Club, maintainers of the A.T. in this area. The new name memorializes his contribution.

The hike starts at the same parking area as the Old Hotel/Appalachian Trail circuit (see that entry). The blue-blazed trail starts in a parking area with an information and map board. The trail enters a "timber regeneration" area that makes for good camping.

At about .5 mile, the trail gains the first crest. Still on the ridge, the trail rises gradually, dips into a gap, then continues up the ridge and passes the

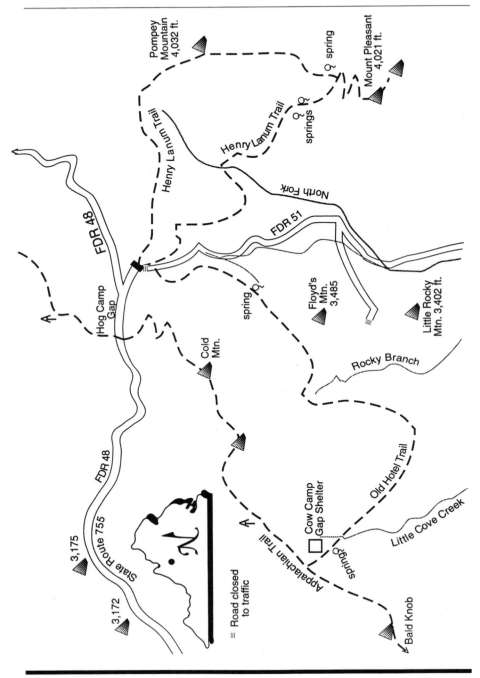

Pompey Mountain 4,032 ft.

spring

Mount Pleasant 4,021 ft.

Henry Lanum Trail

springs

Henry Lanum Trail

North Fork

FDR 51

FDR 48

Hog Camp Gap

spring

Floyd's Mtn. 3,485

Little Rocky Mtn. 3,402 ft.

Cold Mtn.

Rocky Branch

Old Hotel Trail

FDR 48

State Route 755

3,175

3,172

Appalachian Trail

Cow Camp Gap Shelter

spring

Little Cove Creek

= Road closed to traffic

Bald Knob

peak of Pompey Mountain, 4,032 feet, at 1.6 miles. The trail descends from the summit into a large gap between Pompey Mountain and Mt. Pleasant at 2.4 miles. A major side trail heads left to the area's best views. There's also a side path, to the left, that reaches a spring. There are good campsites in the area.

The spur steeply ascends to the main summit of the mountain, giving hikers the most intense workout of the entire trip. The peak is really two crags, each at an end of a summit plateau. Both resemble rocky towers, with interesting cracks to scramble around on. Huckleberries are profuse in late summer.

Interestingly, the forest service says Mt. Pleasant is 4,021 feet high. But topo maps show the measured crag to be the most distant, and lowest of Mt. Pleasant's two crags. The unmeasured peak on the map is surrounded by a higher topo line, suggesting that the first summit reached is up to 59 feet higher than the more distant, measured crag.

Evaluating that discrepancy is a small sidelight to the sweeping views hikers have from this prominent peak. Surrounding topography quickly plummets from the 4,000-foot cone of the peak to elevations of 800 feet and lower. That kind of relief yields dramatic views. The side trip to the peak adds one mile to the hike.

Back at the loop trail, the hike continues with a swing out of the gap to the northwest. At 2.9 miles, hikers will find a spring on the right, and at three miles, there's one on the left. A creek is crossed at about 3.5 miles, and the trail ends back in the parking lot at the five-mile mark.

This is a scenic day hike, and a nice beginner backpacking trip. More experienced packers could figure eight this loop with the Old Hotel/Appalachian Trail circuit for a trip of eleven miles. (The only drawback is that the backcountry atmosphere of the trip is broken in half by walking back past your car.)

# HIKE 21 HUMPBACK ROCKS ON THE APPALACHIAN TRAIL

**General description:** A short hike (one mile, two miles round trip) from the Blue Ridge Parkway, west of Charlottesville, to panoramic views at Humpback Rocks, and two longer hikes (two miles, four miles round trip) to vistas atop Humpback Mountain.

**Elevation gain and loss:** Approximately 1,440 feet to rocks; 2,480 feet to peak.

**Trailhead elevation:** Approximately 2,360 feet.

**High point:** Approximately 3,080 feet at rocks, 3,600 feet at peak.

**Water availability:** Water is available in season at Humpback Rocks Visitor Center, .2 mile north of Humpback Gap trailhead parking, on the Blue Ridge Parkway.

**Finding the trailhead:** The trailhead, at Humpback Gap parking area (Blue Ridge Parkway milepost 6) is six miles south of I-64 and Rockfish Gap on the northernmost section of the Blue Ridge Parkway. Take I-64 eighteen miles west of Charlottesville to exit 19.

**The hike:** This classic Blue Ridge Parkway "leg-stretcher," actually a stretch of the Appalachian Trail, reaches one of the best views in the central Blue

*Table Mountain Pine and hemlocks struggle to survive on a windy crag below Humpback Mountain (background).*

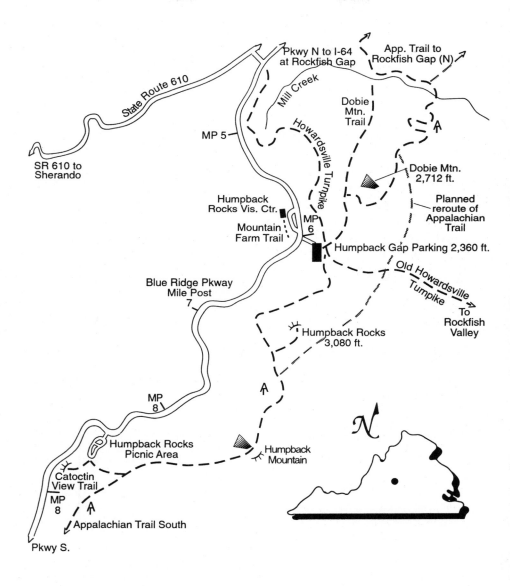

Pkwy N to I-64
at Rockfish Gap

App. Trail to
Rockfish Gap (N)

State Route 610

Mill Creek

Dobie
Mtn.
Trail

MP 5

Howardsville Turnpike

SR 610 to
Sherando

Dobie Mtn.
2,712 ft.

Humpback
Rocks Vis. Ctr.

Planned
reroute of
Appalachian
Trail

Mountain
Farm Trail

MP
6

Humpback Gap Parking 2,360 ft.

Blue Ridge Pkway
Mile Post
7

Old Howardsville
Turnpike

To
Rockfish
Valley

Humpback Rocks
3,080 ft.

MP
8

N

Humpback Rocks
Picnic Area

Humpback
Mountain

Catoctin
View Trail

MP
8

Appalachian Trail South

Pkwy S.

Ridge. The basic hike is the strenuous, one-mile climb to Humpback Rocks, a massive greenstone outcrop at approximately 3,080 feet. The rocks jut west and offer an expansive view up and down the patchwork of Virginia's Shenandoah Valley.

The white-blazed trail leaves the south end of the parking lot at Humpback Gap and ascends in .5 mile to where the old, extremely steep and eroded trail used to go left. (The old trail took a right turn out onto the rocks.) That section was closed in the early 1980s, in favor of the new trail to the right. Unfortunately people still use the old one.

Go right on the newer trail, soon ascending some wooden steps, and follow the path under the rocky crag. The path switchbacks and climbs to a junction, at the mile mark, and a left turn onto Humpback Rocks.

That round-trip is two miles, and if you take your time, it can be a moderate hike. But rangers caution hikers not to forget to turn right when they leave the rocks. Some hikers miss that turn back down the mountain, and unknowingly continue on to the next destination, Humpback Mountain. Searches and unplanned overnight hikes have resulted.

The trip to Humpback Mountain is only another mile, and Appalachian Trail maintainers have been given the okay to clear vistas in the area. The trail continues up the ridgeline, dips into a gap, and then ascends to the summit for 360-degree views. The spine of the Blue Ridge soars north and south, the Shenandoah Valley lies to the west, the rolling Piedmont of Virginia ripples off to the east. The round trip is only four miles.

Those basic hikes are complemented by a few others. To the south of Humpback Mountain, the A.T. leads past the Blue Ridge Parkway's Humpback Rocks Picnic Area (Blue Ridge Parkway milepost 8). A blue-blazed side trail allows hikers to start at the end of the picnic area, beside the Catoctin View Trail, reach the A.T., and hike to Humpback Mountain in about two miles (four miles round trip). That's about the same distance as the hike past Humpback Rocks, but the elevation gain is only 520 feet, less than half the climb from the start of the Humpback Rocks hike.

On the hike to Humpback Mountain from the picnic area, one clifftop view focuses on Wintergreen Resort, a mountaintop golf course and ski resort that has won national awards for its "design with nature" philosophy. The lodge and homes at the resort make a nice base for hikers, especially those sampling the trails in the Humpback Rocks and Crabtree Falls area. The resort's spring Wildflower Symposium, held in mid-May, is known for excellent speakers and guided hikes. Wintergreen's extensive trail system is one of the best resort trail networks in the nation. Views from it reach back to Humpback Mountain and other nearby summits. For information, call or write: Wintergreen Resort, Wintergreen, VA 22958; (800) 325-2200.

There is also interesting hiking north of the Humpback Gap parking area. By heading north on the A.T., hikers have access to an A.T. loop and a side trail that makes a nice out-and-back walk.

Just outside the parking area on the Appalachian Trail north, the Old Howardsville Turnpike goes left (to a junction with the Parkway between mileposts 4 and 5) and right (descending in 3.5 miles to the Rockfish Valley). The historic old road, built between 1846 and 1851, connected the Shenandoah Valley with the James River Canal system that reached Richmond. Ancient rock walls and bridges are part of this trail's appeal to history hikers.

Going north on the A.T., hikers can take a left on a blue-blazed side trail, eventually rejoin the Appalachian Trail and loop back south to the parking area for a hike of about two miles. This hike goes left on the blue-blazed Dobie Mountain Trail, once a section of the Appalachian Trail. It rejoins the new A.T., which creates the loop, and passes a new trail shelter, Mill Creek, a little more than a mile north of the Humpback Gap parking area.

Within the next three years, another reroute of the Appalachian Trail will move other sections of the path farther east, starting from a point south of Humpback Rocks. That is expected to yield another hiking loop in the area, predicted to be about four miles. However, the Appalachin Trail changes are not expected to affect the trail descriptions above. Access to the rocks and Humpback Mountain will still be possible on the "old A.T." In fact, the Park Service expects to maintain the old paths to expand hiking opportunities in the Humpback Rocks area.

Also consider a stop at the Humpback Rocks Visitors Center and sample the .25-mile Mountain Farm Trail (accessible to wheelchairs). The restored cabins and out buildings, and seasonal, costumed interpreters, give startling insight into the life led by Appalachian Mountaineers. This pioneering lifestyle was very much still in existence when the Blue Ridge Parkway penetrated the area in the mid-1930s.

# HIKE 22 *SHARP TOP TRAIL*

**General description:** This steep, 1.5-mile trail leads from the Blue Ridge Parkway's Peaks of Otter camp store to the rocky, spectacular summit of Sharp Top, 3,875 feet.
**Elevation gain and loss:** 2,680 feet.
**Trailhead elevation:** 2,535 feet.
**High point:** 3,875 feet.

*From the Peaks of Otter Visitor Center on the Blue Ridge Parkway, Sharp Top rises into the clouds.*

*The Sharp Top Trail boasts distant views from many crags along the trail between the Blue Ridge Parkway and the summit.*

**Water availability:** Camp store at trailhead has water.

**Finding the trailhead:** The trail is located in Peaks of Otter Recreation Area on the Blue Ridge Parkway between mileposts 84 and 87. Opposite the Peaks of Otter Visitor Center, near milepost 86, park at the camp store, beside which the trail begins.

**For more information:** District Ranger, Blue Ridge Parkway, Route 2, Box 163, Bedford, VA 24523, (540) 586-4357.

**The hike:** This popular trail can be crowded on summer and fall weekends. Part of its popularity stems from the fact that a national park service shuttle bus ferries riders to the summit of Sharp Top for a small fee, making it easy for people to hike down who might not be able to make the climb up (contact the park for current rates and times). The trail isn't long, and even though it is steep, the hike is often made by families and older people.

Sharp Top is one of Virginia's most distinctive summits and a major landmark of the Blue Ridge range. Its prominent conical peak, capped by rounded boulders, is visible from many places in the eastern foothills and can even be seen from the Great Valley side of the mountains. Understandably, the views from the peak survey that same striking domain. That makes it possible

*From Buzzards Roost on the Sharp Top Trail, the Blue Ridge and the Great Valley of Virginia ripple toward the Allegheny Mountains on the distant West Virginia state line.*

to look down on spring greenery from a frosty peak, or still see summer in the valley from amid colorful fall foliage.

The trail switchbacks through a deciduous forest for 1.2 miles before reaching a junction. To the right about .4 mile, a side trail reaches Buzzards Roost, a rocky crag that from different vantage points alternates between looking like a large foot or a dragon's head.

Above the junction, the trail reaches its steepest section, and actually climbs steps cut into solid rock. All of that is just preparation for the summit, a jumble of house-size boulders. Another side path descends to the mountaintop shuttle bus stop, and other highly developed trails lead to viewpoints that take in the entire 360-degree view. A large summit shelter is on hand in case of inclement weather, which can include direct lightning strikes. (No camping in shelter.)

Hikers should retrace their steps downhill on the trail, because no walking is permitted on the road.

Nearby Flat Top, 4,004 feet, is the other summit of the so-called Peaks of Otter. Below lies twenty-four-acre Abbott Lake beside the Peaks of Otter Lodge, a highly recommended base of operations (year-round lodging and dining) that complements a campground, picnic area, service station, visitor center, and restored mountain farm. Except for the lodge, the rest of the facilities are operated by the National Park Service from May through October, with limited winter use of the campground permitted.

Winter access is good because VA 43, the best route from Interstate 81 near Buchanan and route 221 at Bedford, crosses the parkway and actually follows the scenic road for five miles. That makes it necessary for that section of road to be plowed, even when the rest of the Parkway is "closed" due to snowfall.

# HIKE 23 HARKENING HILL, JOHNSON FARM, PEAKS OF OTTER NATURE LOOPS

**General description:** Scenic, short to moderate length interpretive trails that impart a real sense of how the Southern Appalachian mountaineers lived.
**Elevation gain and loss:** 1,628 feet (for Harkening Hill Trail).
**Trailhead elevation:** 2,550 feet.
**High Point:** 3,364 feet.
**Water availability:** Available in season at trailhead visitor facilities and campground, and in the winter at a frostproof spigot in the campground.
**Finding the trailhead:** These trails start at the Peaks of Otter Visitor Center, just north of Blue Ridge Parkway milepost 86.

**The hike:** The Harkening Hill Loop, Johnson Farm Trail, and Elk Run Interpretive Loop Trail start at the Peaks of Otter Visitor Center and range in length from just under a mile to 3.3 miles. Together they offer insight into the lifestyle of Southern Appalachian mountaineers.

The trails begin at the roadside concession/visitor center area. The view from there encompasses the conical peak of Sharp Top and the broader summit of Flat Top. This high valley is a spectacular stop on the Blue Ridge Parkway, but during previous centuries, its isolated wilderness character must have been awe-inspiring.

Archaeological work has established that Indians hunted elk here on the fringe of a boggy meadow that is now the site of Abbott Lake. (The lake was built with Peaks of Otter Lodge in 1964. Today, an effort to flood a similar high mountain bog would almost certainly be stopped by environmentalists, or not even proposed.) The first land was cleared by settlers in 1766, and by the 1830s, an "ordinary" was established near the Peaks of Otter Campground that served people on their way over the Blue Ridge. Tourist hotels, ancestors of the current Peaks of Otter Lodge, opened as early as 1857.

By the 1930s, a community of more than twenty self-reliant, independent families populated the high valley, including the last of the Johnson family

*Peaks of Otter Lodge, from Sharp Top.*

for whom the Johnson Farm Trail is named. A school and church stood near the current site of the Peaks of Otter Lodge. The families were mostly subsistence farmers, but the tourist traffic to the hotel and up the road to the Sharp Top summit supplied cash for those locals who had jobs.

The Depression signaled the end of all that. The Johnson farm was sold in 1941. The house changed hands, was purchased by the National Park Service, and deteriorated until the 1950s when it was stabilized. The house was restored in 1968. Today, the house and related buildings are the heart of what may be the Parkway's best living history exhibit. Throughout the season, visitors can actually participate in the recreated life of the farm.

The Humpback Rocks farm, at Parkway milepost 6, features more rustic, pioneer-like log structures. But the Johnson Farm captures the lifestyle of mountaineers still pioneering just before the Blue Ridge Parkway forever changed life in these high hollows.

The easy to moderate Johnson Farm hike starts at the northern end of the visitor center parking lot. Take the trail toward Peaks of Otter Lodge, but pass the trail that leads right to the lodge. The first trail to the left is also part of the Johnson Farm Loop, but the farm is closer going straight ahead.

The trail enters a dirt road and reaches the farm at just under one mile from the parking area. A quarter mile past the farm, the Harkening Hill Loop comes in on the right. Hikers who take a left and stay on the Johnson Farm Trail return to the trail from the parking lot and return to the visitor center in just under two miles.

The longest walk, with nearly 1,000 feet of elevation gain, is the Harkening Hill Trail, a moderately strenuous path that explores a now wooded area that used to be cultivated fields. From the upper part of the trail, hikers can look down on the Johnson Farm, and take a short spur trail to Balance Rock.

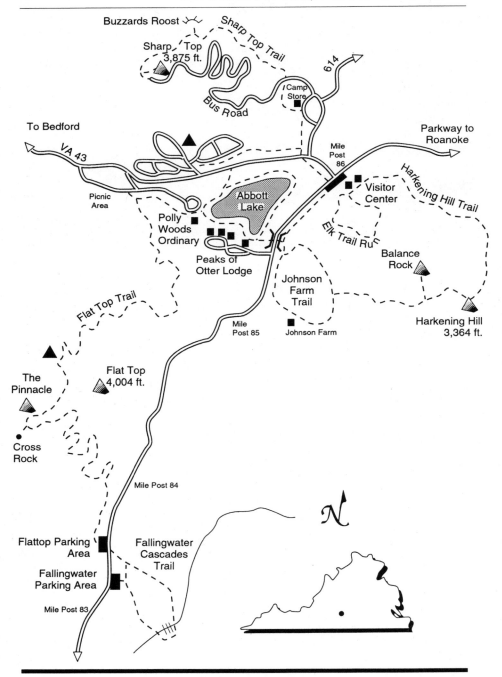

Buzzards Roost

Sharp Top Trail

Sharp Top
3,875 ft.

614

Camp Store

Bus Road

To Bedford

VA 43

Parkway to Roanoke

Mile Post 86

Visitor Center

Harkening Hill Trail

Picnic Area

Abbott Lake

Polly Woods Ordinary

Elk Trail Run

Peaks of Otter Lodge

Balance Rock

Johnson Farm Trail

Harkening Hill 3,364 ft.

Flat Top Trail

Mile Post 85

Johnson Farm

The Pinnacle

Flat Top 4,004 ft.

Cross Rock

Mile Post 84

N

Flattop Parking Area

Fallingwater Cascades Trail

Fallingwater Parking Area

Mile Post 83

The trail leaves the visitor center and climbs a series of ridges, at times steeply, to Harkening Hill. At about the 1.5 mile mark, there is a good, but restricted view. At 1.8 miles, the summit affords a viewpoint, too.

The side trail to Balance Rock, a boulder perched on natural pedestal, heads right at about two miles. At 2.5 miles, the trail joins the Johnson Farm trail. Continuing, the visitor center is reached after 3.3 miles.

The shortest hike is the .8-mile Elk Run Loop Trail, an educational nature trail with interpretive signs. The trail is easy but has numerous ups and downs, and a number of benches.

# Saint Mary's Wilderness

*Entering the Saint Mary's Wilderness on the Mine Bank Trail, a short distance from the Blue Ridge Parkway.*

# HIKE 24 *LOWER SAINT MARY'S WILDERNESS WALKS*

**General description:** The Saint Mary's Trail provides a variety of out-and-back hikes along the cascading Saint Mary's River, centerpiece of the Saint Mary's Wilderness near Staunton. The entire trail creates the area's longest circuit hike, more than seventeen miles, when combined with the Cellar Mountain Trail.

**Elevation gain and loss:** 3,200 feet.
**Trailhead elevation:** 1,760 feet.
**High point:** 3,360 feet.

*Big Spy Mountain (left) and the rest of the Saint Mary's Wilderness summit area from the Blue Ridge Parkway's Big Spy Mountain Trail.*

**Water availability:** The first half of the hike parallels the Saint Mary's River.

**Finding the trailhead:** The trail starts at the end of FDR 41, reached via I-81 from the Raphine exit (exit 54), approximately nineteen miles south of the I-64/I-81 junction near Staunton. Exit the interstate and go east on Virginia 56 in the direction of Steele's Tavern. Turn left onto State Route 608, then turn right onto FDR 41 and follow it to the trailhead parking area.

**The hike:** The 9,835-acre Saint Mary's Wilderness is the largest of Virginia's federal wilderness areas. The tract lies west of the Blue Ridge Parkway, just south of Staunton and the start of the Blue Ridge Parkway near Waynesboro.

The area was never logged, but the rugged slopes and thin soil have not produced a towering virgin forest like the one found in the Ramseys Draft. Nevertheless, the scenery is impressive. Oak and hickory forests predominate, while the summits are covered with pitch pine, table mountain pine, bear oak, and mountain laurel. Large, barren talus fields appear as gray jumbles of rock on otherwise lush, green slopes.

The Saint Mary's Trail follows the Saint Mary's River, with waterfalls and deep pools among the attractions. Large pools below waterfalls, some ten feet deep, attract dippers in the heat of the summer. None of the falls on the Saint Mary's are dramatic, but quartzite cliffs and large streambed boulders make the setting a scenic one.

The wilderness is very popular, especially the lower section of the Saint Mary's River Trail. Regulations prohibit camping around the trailhead parking area, and campfires are banned in the vicinity of the parking area and within 150 feet of the trail from the parking area to beyond the falls, about two miles. During the warmer months and the fall, weekdays are the best time to visit.

The trail emerges from the valley onto a high plateau, and when linked with a jeep road and the Cellar Mountain Trail, adds up to a more than seventeen-mile circuit that is perfect for backpacking.

The gradual trail is easy and was once a railroad grade that served mostly manganese mines that operated from the early 1900's to the 1950's. Today the area is home to deer, turkey, grouse, and a respectable population of black bear. Trout are prevalent in the Saint Mary's River, though that stream was recently found to be among those in the Southern Appalachians where an increase in acidity from "acid rain" and related phenomenon is having a negative impact on at least one species of tiny native fish.

The blue-blazed trail starts at a well-developed trailhead where an information board acquaints hikers with the latest regulations. The path wanders about during the first mile, crossing the river at about 1.2 miles. The crossing can be tricky in very wet weather. A side trail just past that crossing yields a nice view of the river.

At 1.4 miles, the trail turns right to follow Sugar Tree Branch, while a side trail continues for .5 mile on the Saint Mary's River to a waterfall at the base of the Saint Mary's River gorge. The old railroad grade continues past the falls and serves as a bushwhack route back from higher up the stream.

Continuing up the stream, the trail crosses Sugar Tree Branch at 1.7 miles, and enters an open area at 1.9 miles that once was the location of a mining operation. An old mining building still stands at 2.1 miles. At 3.6 miles, the Mine Bank Trail enters from the right. For more information, see the section on the upper Saint Mary's River area.

The Saint Mary's River Trail climbs out of the drainage onto the flat open terrain of Big Levels at 6.3 miles, and at 6.4 miles reaches Green Pond, a scenic, natural pond and a perfect campsite. The forest service asks that all camping in the wilderness be in a no-trace manner, especially at sensitive sites like Green Pond.

At any time during the above hike, you can retrace your steps for a scenic day hike. And from the vicinity of the Mine Bank Trail, you can locate the old railroad grade and bushwhack down the Saint Mary's River to create a change of pace circuit on the upper part of the hike.

The longest hike, and a nice backpacking trip of one or two nights, involves camping at Green Pond, and then continuing past the pond .3 mile to FDR 162, a primitive jeep road that makes an acceptable trail. Take a left and hike northwest on FDR 162. If you go to the right, the road reaches the Blue Ridge Parkway in 3.5 miles and other trails covered under the upper Saint Mary's River area.

Not far from Green Pond, FDR 162 goes right, and hikers bear left on another jeep road, FDR 162-A, sometimes called the Wigwam Road. About 5.5 miles from Green Pond, or 12.2 miles into the hike, go left at the junction of the blue-blazed Cellar Mountain Trail. This old Civilian Conservation Corps-constructed trail crosses Cellar Mountain (3,645 feet) in one of the least-visited parts of the Saint Mary's Wilderness.

The Cellar Mountain Trail, and the nearby Cold Spring Trail, descend to FDR 42. The Cold Spring Trail's present route is interrupted by private property that can be skirted by following the marked forest boundary. The trail passes the quiet valley site of Cold Spring, the location of a rustic resort in the late 1880's, and now a nice campsite. The current U.S. Forest Service map (1990) of the Saint Mary's Wilderness inaccurately depicts the route of the Cold Spring Trail. See Virginia's National Forests for ordering information.

The Cellar Mountain Trail reaches FDR 42 at about fifteen miles. Hikers who parked at the Saint Mary's Trail will have to walk south on FDR 42 to FDR 41, then left to the parking area, a total of another 2.5 miles. That creates a more than seventeen-mile hike.

# HIKE 25  *UPPER SAINT MARY'S WILDERNESS CIRCUIT TO GREEN POND*

**General description:** An eleven-mile loop hike, and a shorter option, from the Blue Ridge Parkway through Saint Mary's Wilderness to scenic Green Pond, a natural, high-elevation pond just south of Shenandoah National Park.
**Elevation gain and loss:** 2,374 feet.
**Trailhead elevation:** 3,294 feet.
**Low point:** 2,200 feet.
**High point:** 3,480 feet.
**Water availability:** Stream is reached two miles into the hike. Blue Ridge Parkway's Humpback Rocks Picnic Area, with restrooms and water, is 14.5 miles north of the trailhead.
**Finding the trailhead:** A gravel side road leaves the Blue Ridge Parkway near milepost 23, opposite the Fork Mountain Overlook. The short gravel road ends at the trailhead. The Blue Ridge Parkway reaches the trail from Rockfish Gap, twenty-three miles north at its intersection with Interstate 64 west of Charlottesville.

**The hike:** The Saint Mary's Wilderness is a popular hiking area, especially at its lowest elevations where trailside waterfalls are an attraction.

Higher up, adjacent to the Blue Ridge Parkway, these hikes offer a combination of streamside and mountaintop scenery, and an absence of crowds. Two circuit hikes offer options of under five miles and more than ten miles. The longer circuit is a nice overnight trip with camping on a stream, or at Green Pond—a rare, natural pond located on an open ridgetop.

The trail starts just a mile from the highest point on the Blue Ridge Parkway north of the James River, 3,333 feet. From the parking area, the orange-blazed Mine Bank Trail enters the wilderness and in 100 yards, the Bald Mountain Trail goes right to FDR 162. The Mine Bank Trail quickly descends north to Mine Bank Creek and follows the stream two miles, dropping nearly 1,100 feet to a junction with the blue-blazed Saint Mary's Trail.

The Saint Mary's Trail runs up and down the stream, but turn right and follow the gradually ascending trail, a railroad grade that once served nearby mines. Cross two creeks to excellent campsites in the vicinity of Bear Branch. The mining that used to take place in the area is visible here at "Red Mountain Mines." There used to be more than twenty buildings, including residences, in this mining community. Foundations are still visible. Local mining focused on coal, iron, and manganese.

The gradual grade of the Saint Mary's Trail continues, then steepens, before leveling out on a ridgetop appropriately named Big Levels. The trail exits the wilderness and reaches Green Pond at about 4.8 miles, a very rare, natural tarn surrounded by pines. Sedges and a colony of cranberry grow in the boggy area. There are excellent campsites by the pond, but camp in a "no-trace"

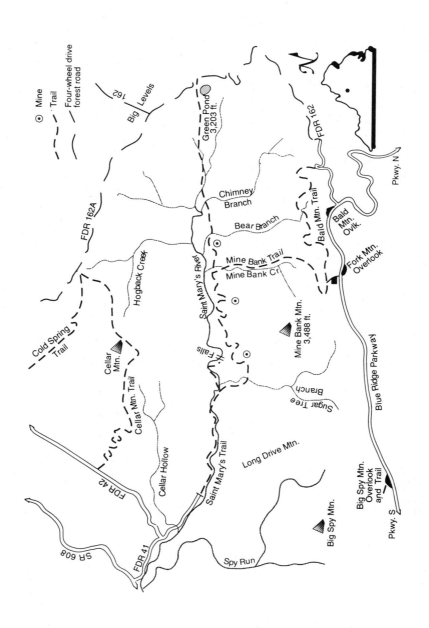

manner. The trail continues .3 mile farther to reach the Stoney Run Jeep Trail (FDR 162) at 5.1 miles.

The jeep trail used to reach the pond, with resulting litter and damage to the fragile, scenic spot. The forest service has rerouted the road away from the pond, making the pond a nicer place to camp and insuring its protection from vehicles. Four-wheelers can still drive nearby, but vehicular access now poses less of a problem than it once did.

Reaching the jeep trail, turn right and hike the primitive road along a gradually ascending ridge for three miles. At about 8.1 miles, turn right on the yellow-blazed Bald Mountain Trail. The trail follows the headwaters of scenic Bear Branch, passes some nice campsites, but then turns out of the stream drainage to ascend and intersect the Mine Bank Trail at about 10.3 miles. Make a left on the Mine Bank Trail, and reach the parking lot. This lengthy hike can be taken in either direction.

It can also be shortened to a less than five-mile loop of the Bald Mountain Trail. Walk north on the Blue Ridge Parkway .9 mile to the Bald Mountain Overlook. Just past the overlook, walk northeast away from the Parkway on FDR 162 and reach the Bald Mountain Trail, on the left, at 1.5 miles. Hike that trail back to your vehicle at the Mine Bank Trail parking area at about 4.8 miles.

These trails offer great hiking and camping options. Campers wanting to quickly reach a secluded Saint Mary's backpacking spot can reverse the directions given above for the Bald Mountain Loop, and very quickly be at campsites in the upper Bear Branch (leave no trace). Hikers could also use either Bald Mountain or the jeep trail to reach the top of rugged drainages that make fine bushwhack hikes.

By walking a little ways south on the Blue Ridge Parkway, hikers have a direct ridgetop bushwhack to Mine Branch Mountain, 3,488 feet. And near that access point, the really wild drainages surrounding Big Spy Mountain offer trailless hikes down to the lower Saint Mary's Trail, with that and the Mine Bank Trail for the return trip.

At Blue Ridge Parkway milepost 26, the Spy Mountain Overlook Trail leads .1 mile to a nice view of the Saint Mary's Wilderness, with a focus on Big Spy Mountain.

# Shenandoah National Park

The East's first national park, Shenandoah opened in 1936 after the then unprecedented purchase of populated private land. Today, the 200,000-acre park consists of uninterrupted forest, in the northernmost portion of the Blue Ridge Mountains. The park is mostly one main ridge, with few mountains to the east or west.

The 105-mile-long Skyline Drive meanders through the park. It is accessible through entrance stations at four points, an arrangement that splits the park into northern, central, and southern sections. A $5 per car fee is charged ($3 a person for bus passengers and motorcyclists).

Shenandoah's 500 miles of trails are popular, in part because of the park's accessibility. Interstate 64 reaches the park from Richmond, Interstate 66 provides access from Washington, D.C., and Interstate 81 runs the western length of Shenandoah in the valley of the same name. Hikers and backpackers intent on solitude will want to focus on weekdays and winter. Try to avoid holidays and weekends in the summer and fall.

The park's appeal rests on the rolling, gentle Appalachian scenery. There are a few truly spectacular places in the park, but a more intimate aesthetic is the norm. However, among the park's hollows, hikers will notice evidence of intensive settlement. Civilization had crept high onto the Blue Ridge by the time the founding of the park was authorized in 1926. Today, substantial parts of the park are returning to near-virgin condition, a fact that sparked wilderness designation for two-fifths of Shenandoah's acreage in 1976.

Nearly a decade of work by the Civilian Conservation Corps in the 1930s has created an impressive system of trails and facilities. There are two visitor centers (Byrd at Big Meadows and Dickey Ridge), four major campgrounds, and seven picnic areas. Lodging can be found at three locations, including the rustic, 100-year-old Skyland Lodge and Conference Center (also Lewis Mountain Cabins and Big Meadows Lodge). The season for the park's developed facilities varies, but generally runs from April and early May through weekends in October.

The Potomac Appalachian Trail Club operates six enclosed, locked trail cabins for rent to the public as backcountry camps. These make fine basecamps for day hiking and are the centerpiece of a great backcountry vacation.

**For information on availability and fees, contact Potomac Appalachian Trail Club, 118 Park Street, SE, Vienna, VA 22180, (703) 242-0315, 7-9 p.m., Monday-Thursday, noon-2 p.m., Thursday and Friday** The PATC, publisher of the recommended hiking maps for the park, also manages seven three-sided Appalachian Trail shelters for overnight camping. The shelters, called huts, are often manned by the club's volunteer caretakers, and a $1 per night fee is charged per camper. Priority is given to Appalachian Trail hikers, and any camper who uses the facilities must be in possession of a three-night backcountry camping permit.

**All backcountry overnight use in the park requires a free permit, available in person at any entrance station, ranger station, self-registration station, by phone or by mail from Shenandoah National Park Headquarters, Route 4, Box 348, Luray, VA 22835.** The permit dates your visit, and documents the number of people in your party and your intended backcountry camping locations. The phone number is listed below.

No designated campsites are available in the backcountry, as they once were, and all campers must melt into the foliage to camp 250 yards away from paved roads, .5 mile from developed park facilities, out of sight of hiking trails and other camping parties, and twenty-five feet from any stream.

There are other restrictions. No campfires are permitted. All campers must use a gas backpacking stove. All dogs must be kept on a leash, and owners are discouraged from taking dogs on trails at all. Other prohibitions include the banning of pets on Stony Man Mountain, Old Rag, the Limberlost Trail and in White Oak Canyon. And no camping is permitted on the summits of Old Rag or Hawksbill mountains, in White Oak Canyon, and elsewhere. Inquire about such closures when you pick up your backcountry permit.

Except for the seven shelters managed as "huts," camping in trail shelters is also prohibited. Unfortunately some of those shelters, such as the "Byrd's Nest" shelters, are attractive stone structures that beg to be used. Nevertheless, only emergency overnight occupancy is permitted. Campers should also take precautions against bears, a large population of which call the park home.

Shenandoah's seasons are attractive. At lofty elevations, such as 3,500-foot Big Meadows, summer weather is much cooler than it is in nearby valleys. Despite that, many of the park's trails lie at lower elevations where Piedmont heat reaches into the backcountry.

Autumn is almost too popular in the park. Traffic on Skyline Drive can be bumper to bumper on weekends, and trails can also be crowded then. Winter is also a popular time in the park. A sizeable dose of snow in January and February makes the park popular with winter hikers and especially cross-country skiers. The central section of the park is quickly plowed for winter use, so a number of the trails in this book are very skiable.

**For further information, write to the above address, or call (540) 999-3483, weekdays, or (540) 999-3500 for a twenty-four-hour recording which includes options for receiving information and camping permits.**

# HIKE 26 *THE PORTAL CIRCUIT HIKES*

**General description:** Two lengthy and strenuous circuit hikes (ten and twenty miles) in the southern section of Shenandoah National Park. The shortest can be a day hike, but both are excellent backpacking trips. (See entry on Shenandoah National Park for more on backcountry camping.)
**Elevation gain and loss:** Approximately 4,000 feet for the shorter loop; about 7,100 feet for the longer loop.
**Trailhead elevation:** Approximately 2800 feet.
**High point:** Approximately 2,900 feet (on the longer loop only).
**Low point:** Approximately 1,200 feet.
**Water availability:** Water is available in season at the park's diverse developed facilities, including Loft Mountain Wayside (gasoline, dining, picnicking) and campground, about 2.5 miles south of the trailhead at Brown Mountain Overlook. Substantial portions of these hikes follow streams (boil or treat water).
**Finding the trailhead:** These hikes start at the Brown Mountain Overlook, Skyline Drive milepost 77. The overlook is approximately twenty-nine miles north of the Skyline Drive/Blue Ridge Parkway junction in Rockfish Gap. The Gap is reached via I-64, about thirteen miles east of the I-81/I-64 junction near Staunton, about eighteen miles west of Charlottesville, and ninety-one miles west of Richmond.

**The hikes:** The less popular southern section of Shenandoah is a nice respite from the busier trails farther north. That is illustrated nicely, especially in winter, by the two loops described here.

From the Brown Mountain Overlook, the ridges of Rocky Mountain, Brown Mountain, and Rockytop form two sides of a large triangular watershed bordered by the Skyline Drive. Big Run drains the multi-thousand-acre area between the Drive and the westerly ridgetops. Where the stream reaches its lowest point in the park, it surges through The Portal, a rocky cleft between Brown Mountain and Rockytop.

Both hikes alternate between following ridgetops and streams. And though neither loop climbs much higher than its starting elevation of about 2,800 feet, the valley drops low enough (1,200 feet) that substantial relief challenges

*The Skyline Drive runs north below Little Stony Man Cliffs.*

hikers. In addition, the ridgetop portions of these trails rise and fall frequently over rocky, rugged terrain. Luckily, valley portions of the hike follow more gradual trails, and at times, fire roads.

The easiest circuit, both for day hikers and backpackers, is the Rocky Mountain/Brown Mountain Loop. Departing Brown Mountain Overlook, hikers drop 400 feet in about .75 mile from the Skyline Drive into the gap that separates Rocky Mountain from the main ridge occupied by the scenic road. In the gap, the blue-blazed Rocky Mountain Run Trail leads left, and is the return route for both hikes.

Continuing to Rocky Mountain (also following blue blazes), the trail gains back the 400 feet it just lost, then undulates across the craggy crest with many fine views. The trail gradually descends past Brown Mountain and down to the Big Run Portal Trail in about 4.5 miles, approximately 5.5 miles from the Skyline Drive.

The shorter hike heads left up the yellow-blazed Big Run Portal Trail, but downstream, and across a bridge, the trail passes through The Portal. Going upstream, Big Run rushes along the trail, actually a fire road. Big pools tempt hikers in the heat of summer. After four stream crossings, which can be difficult in high water, the Rocky Mountain Run Trail goes left. That junction is about a mile from the Brown Mountain Trail, and about 6.3 miles from the Skyline Drive.

In about three miles, the Rocky Mountain Run Trail regains the ridge of Rocky Mountain after a strenuous climb. Hikers turn right, to the Skyline Drive's Brown Mountain Overlook, and a total mileage of just under ten miles.

To add another ten miles to this circuit, and take in the little-visited, talus-strewn crest of Rockytop, hikers turn right at the Big Run Portal Trail after descending from Brown Mountain. The fire road passes through The Portal, and .5 mile from the Brown Mountain junction, the blue-blazed Rockytop Trail goes left.

The trail climbs out of The Portal area with switchbacks, crosses talus slopes, and offers distant views on its way to the blue-blazed Lewis Peak Trail, about 3.5 miles from Big Run Portal Trail and just over nine miles from the Skyline Drive. About two miles after that, the Austin Mountain Trail also heads to the right. Both of these trails lead to isolated, rarely visited summits to the west of the Rockytop Trail (1.1 and two miles, one way, respectively). Both are ridge trails to possible campsites, good views, and solitude.

The Rockytop Trail junctions with the Big Run Portal Trail, which at that point is part of the Big Run Loop Trail. That junction is just under six miles from the start of the Rockytop Trail, and about 11.5 miles from the Skyline Drive. Hikers go left, descending in just over one mile to a junction where the Big Run Loop Trail goes right, and the Big Run Portal Trail heads left. Following that fire road trail downhill for about 3.5 miles, hikers turn right on the Rocky Mountain Run Trail, approximately 16.5 miles from the Skyline Drive.

Back at the Skyline Drive, the longer circuit ends at the twenty mile mark.

# HIKE 26 *THE PORTAL CIRCUIT HIKES*

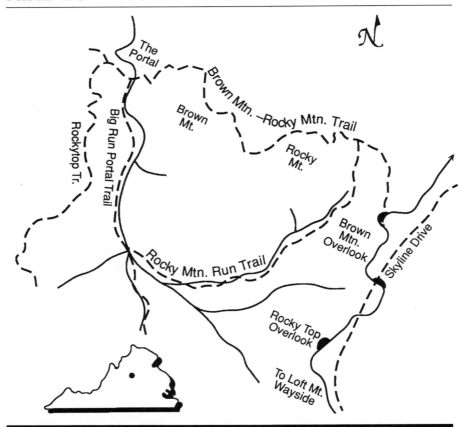

# HIKE 27

## CEDAR RUN/WHITE OAK CANYON CIRCUIT HIKE

**General description:** This is a strenuous, eight-mile hike through some of Shenandoah's deepest, stream-carved canyons. Waterfalls and cascades are abundant.

**Elevation gain and loss:** 4,130 feet.

**Trailhead elevation:** 3,365 feet.

**Low point:** 1,300 feet.

**Water availability:** The trail follows streams. Reliable drinking water is available in season five miles south at Big Meadows concession area, and four miles north, at Skyland concession area.

**Finding the trailhead:** Start at Hawksbill Gap parking area, between Skyline Drive mileposts 45 and 46.

**The hike:** This is an all-day walk deep into the stream gorges formed on the flanks of Shenandoah's loftiest land mass. The scenery is spectacular, in a subtle way. The hike is prone to the sudden sound of cascading water and glimpses of rocky cataracts. Winter is a particularly good time to see these canyons at their icy grandest.

Cross the road from Hawksbill Gap Parking Area and head into the woods on the blue-blazed Cedar Run Trail. Soon the stream of the same name appears on your right. The trail soon begins a consistent descent, and 1.5 miles from the road, crosses to the south side of Cedar Run. From that side, a major waterfall appears. The trail is steep and rocky here. Visible across the gorge is Half Mile Cliff.

A topo map is helpful on this hike, because as the gorge opens up a bit, the route crosses Cedar Run, and can be a bit obscure under heavy autumn leaves or snow. Hikers will want to cross Cedar Run onto the blue-blazed Cedar Run Link Trail, which flattens out and slabs around the intervening ridge to the White Oak Canyon Trail.

The Cedar Run Trail continues on the right side of the stream to a junction with the White Oak Canyon Trail near the Berry Hollow fire road, so if you miss the link, you'll just have a little longer walk.

At about 3.5 miles, the Cedar Run Link Trail crosses the stream into the base of White Oak Canyon. The blue-blazed White Oak Canyon Trail climbs gradually at first, then steepens as the gorge grows sharper. The stream breaks into frequent cascades, eventually reaching a formal waterfall viewpoint. There is impressive stone trailwork in this area.

Above the view, cross the stream to the White Oak fire road at about 5.5 miles, either at a ford, or at the bridge just upstream. The fire road (also a horse trail) crosses the ridge between the two streams, and heads back toward Cedar Run. The fire road eventually veers to the right, toward Skyline Drive, and a horse/foot trail goes left. Head left to reach the Cedar Run Trail .5 mile later. Back at Hawksbill Gap, the total hike is just under eight miles.

Like other sensitive areas of Shenandoah, the steep gorge of White Oak Canyon is a restricted camping area. No camping is permitted between the top of the uppermost waterfall, and the junction of the Cedar Run Link Trail. Pets are not allowed in White Oak Canyon.

# HIKE 28 STONY MAN MOUNTAIN TRAILS

**General description:** An easy nature trail, and steeper, longer hikes lead tothe rocky views of Stony Man Mountain, Shenandoah National Park's second highest peak at 4,010 feet.

**Elevation gain and loss:** 660 feet via the Stony Man Nature Trail; 1,590 feet from Little Stony Man Parking Area on Skyline Drive. Trailhead elevation: 3,680 feet at the nature trail; 3,215 feet at Little Stony Man Parking Area.

**High point:** 4,010 feet.

**Water availability:** Water is available in season at Skyland concession area.

**Finding the trailhead:** The nature trail begins at the first parking area on the right after entering the northern entrance to the Skyland concession area, between Skyline Drive mileposts 41 and 42. The longer hike starts at Little Stony Man Parking Area, north of Skyland, and just south of Skyline Drive milepost 39.

**The hike:** Like Hawksbill, Stony Man's trails offer rocky, open views that are among the best in the park. But unlike Hawksbill, the summit of Stony Man is far easier to reach, especially on the shorter of these two hikes. The nature trail parking area is located very close to the highest point on the Skyline Drive, 3,680 feet, and that makes the climb to the summit an easy one. No pets are allowed.

The peak gets its name because the summit crags resemble a human profile, especially from Stony Man Overlook, between mileposts 38 and 39, on the Skyline Drive north of the mountain. Granted, the "face" is pretty laid back; the "stony man" appears to be on his back looking skyward.

From Skyland, the nature trail is keyed to an interpretive brochure. The easy, 1.5-mile walk climbs and circles the rocky Stony Man summit. The nature trail reaches the peak in .6 miles, and offers the uninitiated a worthwhile introduction to the high-elevation hardwood forest. The path points out the northern red oak, the yellow birch, striped maple, American mountain ash, red spruce, and balsam fir, all trees that cluster where a surprisingly cold Southern climate prompts the start of a transition from hardwoods to a spruce/fir ecosystem.

Old Rag is visible from the nature trail, and gnarled trees near the summit teach a lesson about the harsh winter climate at 4,000 feet. From the summit, the impressive drop to the Shenandoah Valley is much like it was in the late 1800's when George Freeman Pollock opened his road up from the valley and established the Skyland vacation resort. Skyland is still visible from the peak, and continues to attract visitors as a National Park concession with lodging and dining. Thirty years after establishing Skyland, Pollock was instrumental in making the area a national park.

More energetic hikers will want to tackle Stony Man from farther away. There are a few options.

A more strenuous and direct hike to Stony Man starts from north of the peak at the Little Stony Man Parking Area. Hikers can reach the summit using the white-blazed Appalachian Trail, and the blue-blazed Little Stony Man Trail. That 795-foot climb can be as short as 1.9 miles, making a round-trip of 2.8 miles that includes the .4-mile loop around the summit. That trip passes Little

Stony Man Cliffs, one of the best views in the park.

In addition to direct trips to the summit from the nature trail, or Little Stony Man Parking Area, hikers can create circuit hikes from either starting point. The shorter loop, 3.4 miles, starts at the nature trail, loops the summit, descends past Little Stony Man Cliffs and at the A.T., reached in 1.9 miles, heads back to Skyland. When the A.T. reaches the road at Skyland, in 3.2 miles, hikers head left on the road .2 mile to the parking area. That is the easiest direction to make this loop, because the Little Stony Man Trail descends more steeply going north than the A.T. ascends on the return trip south.

The longer loop starts at the Little Stony Man Parking Area. The same loop from there is 4.6 miles due to the half mile A.T. hike from the parking area to the start of the loop.

The least crowded of all these hikes is the .8-mile walk to Little Stony Man Cliffs from the Little Stony Man Parking Area. The 1.6 mile round-trip avoids the more popular top of the mountain, and still offers spectacular views.

# HIKE 29   *OLD RAG CIRCUIT HIKE*

**General description:** A strenuous, up to 7.2-mile circuit hike over one of Virginia's most spectacular, alpinelike summits.
**Elevation gain and loss:** 4,340 feet.
**Trailhead elevation:** 1,100 feet.
**High point:** 3,268 feet.
**Water availability:** Springs at three locations on the Ridge Trail, and at Old Rag Shelter on the Saddle Trail
**Finding the trailhead:** About 8.5 miles south of Sperryville, Virginia (via Routes 522 and 231), turn right onto VA 60 2 at the Hughes River; the turn is just under thirteen miles north of the US 231/29 junction in Madison, Virginia. The main road stays south of the stream, becoming VA 707, and then VA 600. It passes through the tiny village of Nethers, becomes narrower, and ascends to a gate, where the trail starts.

**The hike:** Old Rag is easily among Virginia's most scenic summits, which draws crowds during weekends, holidays, and fall. But don't let that discourage you. Plan to sneak up between the crush of people who hike at the busy times, and you won't be disappointed. Pets are not allowed.

On VA 600, about a mile before the gate where the road ends, you will find a huge, overflow parking area on the left. Beyond the gate, the Weakley Hollow fire road is a nice ski tour or easy walk, and most Old Rag hikers return using that route. The Ridge Trail is the preferred path to the top, and that begins on the left. Area parking utilizes a variety of spaces bordering the road. A backcountry permit self-registration station is at the trailhead. Regulations prohibit pets and camping above 2,800 feet.

Old Rag's billion-year-old jumbled dome of granite is the key to its popularity. Though you won't find evergreens clustered around the crags, the peak's rocky summit gives it an almost alpine feel. The lengthy stretch of rock on the ridge trail offers great views, both to the main ridge of the park, on the west, and to the Piedmont, on the east.

The blue-blazed Ridge Trail passes a spring and switchbacks up through a hardwood forest, emerging onto open rock. The rocky scramble can be slick

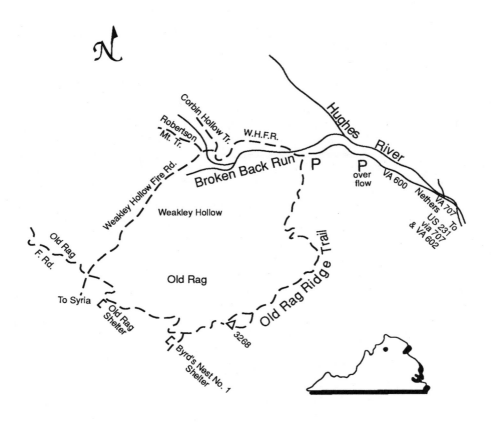

in wet and snowy weather, so use caution. The trail goes through a fissure where softer rock has weathered away, leaving vertical walls and a sloping footway. The trail squeezes through a tunnel and generally follows the massive granite boulders until you reach the summit, 3,268 feet, just under three miles from the start of the trail. There is a spring in the vicinity of the summit, and the respectable rise above the valleys makes for impressive views.

Descending off the other side, the Ridge Trail steps down 300 feet in elevation to the flat site of Byrd's Nest #1, a classic stone shelter (no camping) built

*The rounded, boulder-strewn summit of Old Rag appears stark with light snow falling in Shenandoah National Park. By spring 1996, a hiker permit/rationing system is expected to be in place on Old Rag.*

by the late Senator Harry F. Byrd, Sr. The Saddle Trail drops west from there, descending past a nice view on the way down to the rustic Old Rag Shelter (no camping), where a spring is located.

From the shelter, a fire road descends to a crossroads junction. The Berry Hollow fire road heads left, the Old Rag fire road goes straight, and the Weakley Hollow fire road goes right, returning to the parking area. The junction is about 4.5 miles from the start of the hike.

From the Weakley Hollow fire road junction, it is about 2.5 miles back to the trailhead, and 3.5 miles to the overflow mega-lot. The road has nice views of the peak, and inviting hemlocks shelter tumbling Brokenback Run. Under six or eight inches of snow, the Weakley Hollow fire road makes a fine cross-country ski tour all the way to a lunch break at Old Rag Shelter.

The shortest hike to the Old Rag summit—2.7 miles, 5.4 round-trip is via the Berry Hollow fire road. Hikers who use this route miss the Ridge Trail, though. To hike the mountain this way, continue on VA 231, 2.2 miles south of the VA 601 turn off to Nethers, and turn onto VA 643 at Etlan. Go 4.5 miles and then turn right onto VA 600. The parking area is five miles farther, at the park boundary.

# HIKE 30 *LIMBERLOST*

**General description:** An easy, 1.2 mile-trail through towering hemlocks.
**Elevation gain and loss:** 300 feet.
**Trailhead elevation:** 3,370 feet.
**Low point:** 3,220 feet.
**Water availability:** Available in season at Skyland concession area, .5 mile to the north on the Skyline Drive.
**Finding the trailhead:** Park at Skyline Drive milepost 43, at the entrance to the Old Rag fire road.

**The hike:** The Limberlost Trail is appropriately named. The easy path wanders through impressive groves of virgin hemlocks, easily the largest such stand in the park. This is indeed a parklike setting, one that can be enjoyed by children and older hikers, and especially cross-country skiers.

Park in the entrance for the Old Rag fire road at Skyline Drive milepost 43. Turn right onto the Limberlost Trail from the fire road. The gradual trail drops a little in this area. Bear left when the Crescent Rock Trail branches right, and continue on to a junction with the White Oak Canyon Trail. Take that trail left to the Old Rag fire road, then go left to the parking area on Skyline Drive. Hikers can also continue past the White Oak Canyon Trail to the Old Rag fire road, and then follow that route back to the Skyline Drive.

A longer, more strenuous, but still moderate hike is possible from the White Oak Canyon Trail Parking Area, .5 mile north of milepost 43, opposite the southern entrance to Skyland.

By taking the White Oak Canyon Trail, hikers can add about a mile to the Limberlost, making it a little more than two miles. To do so, follow the White Oak Canyon Trail .5 mile to the Old Rag fire road, then go right to the start of the Limberlost Trail near the parking area at milepost 43. Make the Limberlost loop as above, and just return via the White Oak Canyon Trail. That longer hike adds about 150 feet of descent and 150 feet of ascent to the 300 feet of gain and loss already found on the shorter hike.

The Limberlost is one of the areas in Shenandoah National Park where backcountry camping and pets are not permitted.

# HIKE 31 *HAWKSBILL MOUNTAIN HIKE*

**General description:** A moderate, 2.7-mile circuit hike to the highest peak in Shenandoah National Park, Hawksbill Mountain, 4,051 feet.
**Elevation gain and loss:** 1,372 feet.
**Trailhead elevation:** 3,365 feet.
**High point:** 4,051 feet.
**Water availability:** Spring .3 mile from trailhead.
**Finding the trailhead:** Trail starts at Hawksbill Gap Parking Area on Skyline Drive, between mileposts 45 and 46.

*From the snowy summit of Hawksbill Mountain, the Skyline Drive runs north with the Blue Ridge through Shenandoah National Park. Old Rag rises on the right.*

**The hike:** Hawksbill's status as the park's highest peak is enough to make it a worthwhile walk. But the surrounding terrain, which plummets a dramatic 2,500 feet into Timber Hollow and more than 3,000 feet to nearby Luray, adds to the hiker's pleasure. That relief is the most dramatic drop in the park.

An observation platform caps the peak and permits nearly 360- degree views. The scenes to the north, toward Stony Man Mountain, and to the west, toward the patchwork quilt of the Shenandoah Valley, are truly inspiring. In winter, Hawksbill is often snowy, and coated in hoarfrost by passing clouds.

The blue-blazed trail starts off steep and passes a spring in the first .3 mile. You attain the summit in .8 mile, after a reasonably strenuous climb. The summit flat is the site of Byrd's Nest #2 (no camping), a scenic stone shelter

## CEDAR RUN/WHITE OAK CANYON CIRCUIT HIKE;
## STONY MAN MOUNTAIN TRAILS;
## THE LIMBERLOST;
## HAWKSBILL MOUNTAIN HIKE

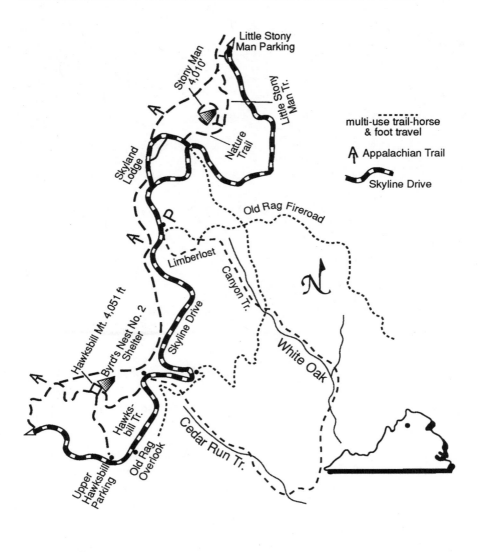

Little Stony Man Parking

Stony Man 4,010'

Little Stony Man Tr.

Nature Trail

Skyland Lodge

Old Rag Fireroad

Limberlost

Canyon Tr.

N

Skyline Drive

White Oak

Hawksbill Mt. 4,051 ft

Byrd's Nest No. 2 Shelter

Hawks-bill Tr.

Old Rag Overlook

Upper Hawksbill Parking

Cedar Run Tr.

multi-use trail-horse & foot travel

A Appalachian Trail

Skyline Drive

built by the same Virginia senator who funded the other two "Byrd's Nests" in the park, including one on Old Rag. Camping is not permitted on the summit of the mountain. Backpackers should determine where they'll camp in the vicinity after discussing the latest regulations with the ranger who issues the required overnight backcountry permit.

A line of cliffs runs across in front of the shelter, offering great views into the Shenandoah Valley and across to the Allegheny Front. An observation area sits on the northernmost prow of the peak, below which the crags decline to wooded cliffs and scree slopes. Among the hardwoods, you'll notice some of Shenandoah's few spruce and fir trees.

The quickest route back to the car, less than a mile, is a descent of the trail you took to the top. A two-mile exit continues on the Hawksbill Trail, generally following the cliff line near the shelter as it diminishes to the southwest. Don't mistakenly follow the fire road, which eventually reaches the Skyline Drive at milepost 47.

The Hawksbill Trail switchbacks a little, drops 400 feet, and reaches a junction with the Appalachian Trail after .9 mile. Turn right onto the white-blazed A.T., which goes east for one mile back to the Hawksbill Gap parking area.

Once on the A.T., the hiker will soon see the Naked Top trail, which takes off to the north. The less than .5-mile Naked Top Trail reaches, and then makes a short loop around, the top of Naked Top. Total round-trip is about .8 mile, with good views in the winter.

Continuing down the A.T., the gradually descending trail slabs across the north face of Hawksbill. Scree slopes climb to cliffs above the trail, giving a feeling of rugged openness. Near Hawksbill Gap, a side trail leaves the A.T. and reaches the Skyline Drive.

Cross-country skiers will enjoy Hawksbill most from the Upper Hawksbill Parking Area, between mileposts 46 and 47. There an easy trail connects to the fire road that climbs to the vicinity of the shelter on the summit. The trail is easy, out and back to the fire road, and intermediate up to the summit and back.

# Central Blue Ridge Mountains

# HIKE 32  OLD HOTEL/APPALACHIAN TRAIL CIRCUIT

**General description:** A moderate, six-mile circuit hike in the central Blue Ridge that follows the Appalachian Trail and the newly opened Old Hotel Trail. The circuit is adjacent to the Henry Lanum Trail (formerly Pompey and Mt. Pleasant Loop Trail) and together they offer highly recommended day and overnight hiking options.

**Elevation gain and loss:** Approximately 2,208 feet.

**Trailhead elevation:** Approximately 3,435 feet.

**High point:** 4,022 feet at Cold Mountain.

**Low point:** Approximately 3,040 feet.

**Water availability:** Springs are located on the trail at .8, 1.0, and 2.8 miles.

**Finding the trailhead:** The trail starts at a major trailhead parking area, just under five miles from U.S. 60 via State Routes 634 and 755, and FDRs 48 and 51. Reach the trailhead by taking U.S. 60 west from Amherst (about fifteen miles north of Lynchburg, and about forty-five miles south of exit 22 on I-64 near Charlottesville). From U.S. 60, about 18.3 miles west of Amherst, turn right onto State Route 634. Then turn right onto State Route 755, and continue on FDR 48 when state maintenance ends. Reach Hog Camp Gap, the Appalachian Trail crossing, and proceed the last .5 mile to the trailhead on FDR 51.

From January to March, the road is gated at the AT crossing, requiring hikers to walk to the trailhead.

**The hike:** The newly opened Old Hotel Trail creates a circuit hike out of one of the nicest central Blue Ridge sections of the Appalachian Trail. There is substantial historic insight and great views to be gained on this trail.

Consider combining this circuit with the Henry Lanum Loop for a lengthier trip (see that entry). This and the Lanum Loop are nice places to avoid the crowds on popular nearby trails. Starting at the main trailhead, also the start of the Henry Lanum Loop Trail, head west on the blue-blazed trail down an old farm road, then south through a vehicle barrier.

At .3 mile, a stream begins on the left, and at .8 mile, the remains of the "Old Hotel" lie entangled in a thicket. This old wooden building probably wasn't a real hotel, just shelter for herders and hunters. A side trail to the left reaches a spring that served the "hotel."

A spring is crossed at about one mile, and the trail meanders between old farm roads and sections of path in this area. At 1.3 miles, the trail enters a stand of young Virginia pine reclaiming a landslide caused by Hurricane Camille in 1969.

This is as good a place as any, especially if it's raining, to ponder that natural disaster. The landmark hurricane hit this particular part of the mountains, the area of the Tye River, harder than anywhere else in the state. More than twenty-five inches of rain fell in five hours. The state, with more than one hundred bridges and 900 buildings swept away, was declared a disaster area. One hundred and fourteen people died, thirty-seven remain missing.

At about 1.5 miles, pre-Civil War stone fences are visible east of the trail. More stone fences are visible at 2.1 miles. Some of these fences are in good condition, despite having been built almost a century and a half ago by slaves. The enclosures, called Hog Walls, were used to pen hogs under the massive chestnuts that once grew here. The animals would fatten-up on the nuts in the fall, prior to being slaughtered. Twelve miles of these walls have been located in the area.

At 2.6 miles, the trail drops across Little Cove Creek. An impressive stand of virgin hardwood forest is located one mile downstream. That drainage intersects gated portions of FDR 51, which leads back to the parking area, so the virgin forest bushwhack could become part of a little traveled loop hike.

A spring and wildlife water hole are on the left at 2.8 miles, and not far ahead, the Old Hotel Trail ends at the Appalachian Trail side trail that reaches Cow Camp Gap shelter and a spring. The shelter and an adjacent tent camping area are about 2.9 miles from the parking area.

The shelter access trail leads to the white-blazed Appalachian Trail in .5 mile. At the A.T., Cow Camp Gap, head right up the prominent ridge of Cold Mountain, labeled Cole Mountain on topo maps. About .8 mile from Cow Camp Gap, and 3.7 miles from the trailhead, the A.T. reaches the spectacular open summit of Cold Mountain, one of the highest peaks in the central Blue Ridge at 4,022 feet. The view is 360 degrees.

The A.T. drops off the summit to the north and makes its way to Hog Camp Gap on a variety of interconnecting dirt roads and paths. At the gap, 5.5 miles from your start, follow the blue-blazed trail east .5 mile to the Old Hotel Trail parking area. The total circuit is about six miles.

# HIKE 33  *CRABTREE FALLS*

**General description:** A moderate three-mile (six-mile round-trip) hike north of Lynchburg that parallels spectacular cascades of statewide significance. A great spring hike after rainfall.

**Elevation gain and loss:** Approximately 3,000 feet.

**Trailhead elevation:** Approximately 1,550 feet.

**High point:** Approximately 3,050 feet.

**Water availability:** The trail follows stream, and a water fountain is available in season at trailhead toilet facilities. A campground, stores, and other water sources are located 3.5 miles west of the trailhead at Montebello.

**Finding the trailhead:** The trail starts on VA 56, east of the Blue Ridge Parkway, north of Lynchburg and southwest of Charlottesville. Reach VA 56 via US 29, about eleven miles north of Amherst and about thirty-four miles south of exit 22 on I-64 near Charlottesville. Follow VA 56 about ten miles to Massies Mill. The trail begins just under 9.5 miles past Massies Mill, on the left, and 6.6 miles east of the Blue Ridge Parkway.

**The hike:** The superlatives lavished on waterfalls are like advertising claims for roadside attractions: they seem designed to impress and not necessarily inform. Various publications describe Crabtree Falls as "the highest in Eastern America," the "highest in Virginia," and the "highest in the Virginia Blue Ridge." Which of those claims to believe is probably dependent on a list of qualified terms and arguable assumptions too lengthy to be juggled here.

What is pertinent is that the Crabtree Falls Trail follows Crabtree Creek during a descent of 1,500 feet to the Tye River, and along the way, there are five major cascades that are indeed spectacular. Chances are they qualify for at least "highest in the Virginia Blue Ridge" status. All of that will be academic to the "oohing" and "aahing" hikers who try this trail.

Starting at VA 56, hikers are in for a climb, but this trail is highly developed and gradual over its entire length. Recent renovation has upgraded the trail, particularly the lower section, so hikers, and even the disabled, who want a short out-and-back walk will find it an easy undertaking.

Parking, restrooms, and a water source mark the start of the hike. The path crosses an impressive bridge spanning the Tye River and then climbs stone steps with hand rails and other improvements. The meandering, defined path is intended to keep you on the trail for good reason. This beautiful cascade has taken twenty-one lives, all people who thought they could scramble to the edge without falling. Watch children closely. This isn't a dangerous trail, as long as hikers stay away from the waterfall.

Developed observation areas overlook the falls at four places along the trail, the last one at about 1.5 miles. A return from that point is a nice three-mile hike. Continuing further, the trail reaches an upper trailhead at State Route

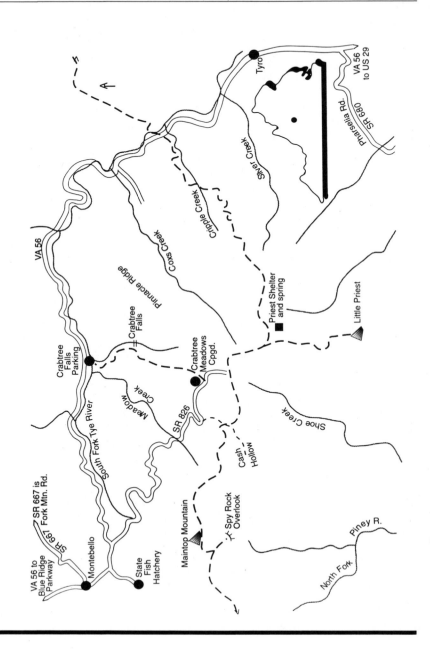

826, an unpaved road that is suitable for use by standard automobiles in good weather. To reach that trailhead, go west from the VA 56 trailhead toward the Blue Ridge Parkway 2.8 miles to a left turn onto State Route 826. The upper trailhead is on the left, about four miles via 826, at Crabtree Meadows, a national forest campground where water is available.

Keep this trailhead in mind for summer and fall weekends when the lower trailhead may be jammed. The best cascade may actually be an easier hike starting from the top. With two cars, there are a number of options, and by parking at the top, a descent of the trail is a very easy walk.

The Appalachian Trail is only .5 mile beyond the upper trailhead, via State Route 826, so hikers and even backpackers can create a spectacular circuit hike over The Priest, 4,063 feet (see that entry). The total length of that hike is just over nine miles. Luckily, the hike up Crabtree Falls Trail is gradual, so backpackers who take their time shouldn't be too taxed. The AT descends to VA 56, 4.7 miles east of the lower Crabtree Falls trailhead.

# Appalachian Trail

Nearly a quarter of the 2,144-mile Appalachian Trail lies in the state of Virginia. That almost 500-mile path offers weeks of wilderness walking through some of Eastern America's most magnificent scenery.

If you hiked the entire length of the trail in Virginia, you'd wind your way through a number of the areas included in this book. The National Scenic Trail seems to cross many of the state's scenic high points.

Many other portions of the trail aren't noted for their scenic beauty. And as an "end-to-end" route, the venerable "A.T." often requires two cars. These considerations focus attention on the most scenic stretches of trail, or on those areas where loop hikes are possible.

Nevertheless, there are a number of places where hikers might want to focus solely on the Appalachian Trail, or create lengthy circuit hikes. The Mount Rogers area, near Abingdon, is a prime example, as is the area of Big Tinker Mountain and the Dragons Tooth, north of Blacksburg. There are various fine sections of the Appalachian Trail adjacent to the Blue Ridge Parkway, particularly a few stretches southwest of Charlottesville in the vicinity of The Priest. Shenandoah National Park is a prized portion of the trail, and that will be obvious to hikers, except perhaps in the winter and on off-season weekdays.

Popularity is the key to consideration of the Appalachian Trail. The most scenic portions are prone to crowding, especially in the summer and fall, and around the three-sided shelters that have come to symbolize the trail. For that reason, backpackers should coordinate an AT hike with other trails and plan to camp in a tent so the truly long-distance hikers can rely on the convenience of a roof over their heads.

Of course, you can be alone on the trail, and have the shelter to yourself, if you choose the right area and the right time to go. If solitude is your goal, go out of your way to satisfy the above two conditions and you won't be disappointed. A thorough reading of the three Appalachian Trail guides (Central and Southwestern VA/ Maryland and Northern VA/ Shenandoah National Park) that cover the state can help you find those special spots.

But overall, the AT experience is often a social one. That dictates that AT hikers wanting solitude take a little extra time to camp well off the trail. It also suggests that precautions should be taken to insure that drinking water is safe.

Though the thought is unpleasant, the trail's popularity dictates that security be given consideration. Experienced AT hikers suggest that trail users never hike alone, that they leave their trip itinerary with friends or family, and that they don't divulge too much about their plans or possessions to strangers. Don't dress to attract attention, and camp where casual visitors won't encounter you. That usually means far from roads and well off the trail. Lastly, leave nothing of value in unattended vehicles, and if you can, be dropped off and picked up.

Despite these sobering cautions, an AT trek can be the trip of a lifetime, even if it's only four or five days long. When Congress passed the National Trails System Act in 1968, designating the AT and Pacific Crest Trail as National Scenic Trails, the intent was to protect an important part of our recreational and natural heritage. In fact, the trail became a linear national park and money was authorized to finally purchase the route or otherwise permanently protect it.

The trail was completed in 1937, just sixteen years after Benton MacKaye suggested the path in a magazine article. Since then, the National Trail System Act, amendments, and experience have helped the National Park Service, U.S. Forest Service, states, and Appalachian Trail Conference hiking clubs forge a system of management that is very close to finalizing a stable, protected route for the trail. That was a fitting achievement to celebrate in 1992, the path's 50th anniversary.

The volunteer basis of the trail's success means that the task of maintaining the trail will never be finished, and the final completion of the path will never be achieved. That provides a fine opportunity for trail enthusiasts to join with any of the ten clubs that maintain the trail in Virginia and have an impact on its appearance and preservation. You needn't live in the mountains. Some clubs are based near the coast.

Whichever portion of the trail you choose to hike, you'll be following the classic blazes of white paint. Other tools include the Appalachian Trail Conference Guides mentioned above, and the maps that come with those books.

The guides cost very close to $20 a piece, but the Central and Southwestern Virginia Guide will be split in late 1993, and that will lower the price. The AT maps that come with the books can also be bought separately, and they include ranger district maps of central and southwestern Virginia published by the U.S. Forest Service and the ATC, and maps published by the Potomac Appalachian Trail Club for Shenandoah National Park and northern Virginia.

All these maps can be ordered by mail. The PATC maps of Shenandoah (about $7) can be ordered from that organization (see the entry for Shenandoah National Park for ordering address.) The ranger district maps can be ordered from any of the organizations. They are available singly (about $4) from the individual ranger districts in central and southwestern Virginia (see forest service addresses under **Virginia National Forests**). The district maps are available from the ATC address in a block of all five, for $19.50.

**For more information, contact: The Appalachian Trail Conference, P.O. Box 807, Washington & Jackson Streets, Harpers Ferry, WV 25425-0807, (304) 535-6331**

# HIKE 34 APPALACHIAN TRAIL TO SPY ROCK

**General description:** A 3.9-mile (7.8-mile round-trip) moderately strenuous day hike on the Appalachian Trail to Spy Rock, perhaps the best viewpoint in the central Blue Ridge.

**Elevation gain and loss:** Approximately 2,600 feet.

**Trailhead elevation:** Approximately 3,050 feet.

**High point:** Approximately 4,020 feet.

**Water availability:** On this hike, water is available only at the trailhead. Other nearby sources include a campground and stores in Montebello, .7 mile west of VA 56/State Route 826 junction on the way to the trailhead.

**Finding the trailhead:** This hike starts at Crabtree Meadows Campground, about twenty-seven miles west of Colleen (located on U.S. 29). From Colleen (about eleven miles north of Amherst, and thirty-four miles south of exit 22 on I-64 near Charlottesville), go west on VA 56 just over twenty-three miles to a left turn on State Route 826. The campground parking area is about four miles further on State Route 826.

**The hike:** Spy Rock may be the single most spectacular viewpoint in the central Virginia Blue Ridge. The outcrop, located on the southeast side of Maintop Mountain, provides a 360-degree view of the convoluted summits that carry this lofty part of the Appalachian Trail. Among the peaks visible are The Priest, The Friar, The Cardinal, Cold Mountain, Pompey Mountain, and Mount Pleasant.

The trail starts at the Crabtree Meadows Campground, also the starting point for a hike to the Priest (see that entry). The hike follows the roughest portion of State Route 826 south from the parking area about .5 mile to the Appalachian Trail. With a right turn on the white-blazed A.T., hikers ascend a ridge with good views and then cross a peak. The trail descends to Cash Hollow, about 1.4 miles from Crabtree Meadows. To the right, the very rough Cash Hollow Road leads to State Route 826, at a point 3.3 miles from VA 56. Hikers could park there, and hike to the A.T. at Cash Hollow in about .25 mile.

From Cash Hollow, the trail climbs a leading ridge of Maintop Mountain (4,040 feet). The forested summit is 2.2 miles from Cash Hollow (about 3.6 miles from Crabtree Meadows). A side trail a short distance past the summit turns right, leading to a view.

Dropping off the summit, the A.T. reaches a small gap south of Maintop Mountain. The Appalachian Trail veers right and a side trail branches left. The side trail follows the ridge less than .1 mile to a cap of crags called Spy Rock, a startlingly good view and a great lunch spot. Spy Rock is about 3.9 miles from Crabtree Meadows, a round-trip of just under eight miles.

Be aware that the Maintop Mountain, Spy Rock area of this hike is private property and no camping is recommended from about the three mile mark.

# HIKE 35 *THE APPALACHIAN TRAIL OVER THE PRIEST*

**General description:** A nine-mile, strenuous day or overnight trip (when combined with the Crabtree Falls Trail) that requires two cars, and features a traverse of The Priest, one of the most scenic summits in the central Virginia Blue Ridge.

**Elevation gain and loss:** 5,579 feet.

**Trailhead elevation:** Approximately 1,550 feet at Crabtree Falls trailhead, approximately 3,050 feet at Crabtree Meadows.

**High point:** 4,063 feet at The Priest.

**Low point:** 997 feet at Appalachian Trail parking on VA 56.

**Water availability:** The start of this hike follows a stream, and a water fountain is available in season at the Crabtree Falls trailhead toilet facilities. Water is also available at Crabtree Meadows and a spring at The Priest Shelter.

**Finding the trailheads:** This hike starts at the Crabtree Falls trailhead (see that entry). It can also start at Crabtree Meadows, (see body of Crabtree Falls entry, or trailhead location under entry for Spy Rock). This hike ends, or can start at the Appalachian Trail parking area on VA 56, twelve miles west of Colleen (on US 29). Colleen is about eleven miles north of Amherst, and thirty-four miles south of exit 22 on I-64 near Charlottesville.

**The hike:** The Priest (4,063 feet) is the highest point in The Religious Range, a series of summits that include The Friar, Little Friar, and The Cardinal. The views in this area are indeed inspiring.

*The Priest viewed from the Blue Ridge Parkway.*

The best circuit requires two cars, and can be as long as nine miles if you start at the Crabtree Falls trailhead. The trip can be shortened with a start at Crabtree Meadows, that also reduces the elevation gain by 1,500 feet. Those are the recommended starting points, because the Appalachian Trail is the preferable route down from The Priest to VA 56. You could climb that section, but the more than 3,000-foot elevation change is steep and strenuous.

The hike starts with the Crabtree Falls Trail (see that entry). To shorten the hike by three miles (for an approximately six mile hike) start at Crabtree Meadows (see body of Crabtree Falls entry, or trailhead location under entry for Spy Rock), a national forest campground reached from State Route 856. You can drive past the campground .5 mile to the junction of the A.T., but parking at the campground has its advantages, including greater public scrutiny of your car and a quicker egress at the end of the day.

The roadside walk from Crabtree Meadows to the A.T. is just under .5 mile. At the Appalachian Trail (about 3.5 miles from the Crabtree Falls trailhead), turn left on the white-blazed trail and begin ascending the leading ridge to The Priest.

At about 1.4 miles (from Crabtree Meadows, 4.4 from Crabtree Falls trailhead) a blue-blazed trail leads right .1 mile to The Priest Shelter and a spring. Continue ascending, and not far past the turn-off to the shelter, notice a side trail to the left that leads to a rocky viewpoint. Continuing, about .5 mile past the shelter, hikers reach the elongated, wooded summit of The Priest (1.9 miles from Crabtree Meadows, 4.9 miles from Crabtree Falls trailhead).

Don't pass this area too quickly. Less than obvious side paths reach nice views and established campsites. Day hikers could turn around at this point, creating a nice four-mile round-trip hike from Crabtree Meadows.

From the summit, the A.T. drops off the mountain steeply in one of the trail's major descents in the Old Dominion. Switchbacks are frequent, and there is a nice view of the Tye River Valley about 3.5 miles from Crabtree Meadows (6.5 miles from Crabtree Falls trailhead). The A.T. reaches VA 56 about six miles from Crabtree Meadows, and about nine miles from the Crabtree Falls trailhead. West on VA 56, the Crabtree Falls trailhead is 4.7 miles away. The Crabtree Meadows trailhead is about 11.5 miles from the VA 56 A.T. parking.

---

# Holliday State Park

# HIKE 36 *HOLLIDAY LAKE LOOP TRAIL*

**General description:** A moderate, 4.6-mile loop trail encircling a wildlife-rich lake in the Piedmont near Appomattox Court House National Historical Park.

**Elevation gain and loss:** Negligible.

**Trailhead elevation:** 500 feet.

**Water availability:** Available in season at the park's diverse developed facilities. Water is available in winter.

**Finding the trailhead:** The park is located in Appomattox County, east of Appomattox on VA 24, then right for eight miles on State Route 626, left on 640 for a short distance, and then right on 692 for three miles. Parking for the longest hike is best from the Saunder's Creek Trail, reached in Campground A. The quickest hike around the lake starts at the swimming beach parking area.

**For more park information, contact:** Holliday Lake State Park, Route 2, Box 622, Appomattox, VA 24522-9802, (804) 248-6308.

**The hike:** The centerpiece of Holliday Lake State Park is a 113-acre lake, reputed to be one of the cleanest bodies of water in the state. The crystal clear water supports wetlands, a diverse population of stocked fish, beavers, great blue herons, and other wildlife. Instead of an interpretive nature trail for hikers, the park has a canoeists nature trail that follows the shoreline near the hiking trail that circles the lake.

The state park is surrounded by the scenic rolling hills of the multi-thousand-acre Appomattox-Buckingham State Forest. The forest managed for wildlife, hunting, timber production, and research contains four significant natural areas that are marked for visitor access but lack extensive trails. There are indications that a twelve-mile trail is now being planned that will link Appomattox National Military Park and Holliday Lake State Park, with much of that trail mileage passing through the surrounding state forest.

The best bet for hiking is the lakeshore path, a nearly five-mile hike if the hiker starts at the Saunder's Creek Trail. This is rated as a moderate hike, due mostly to its length.

The park's pristine lake got its start in the 1930s when efforts were made to help farmers increase the productivity of farmland. Research showed the land to be unsuitable for farming, so the Federal Resettlement Administration acquired the land now included in the forest and state park to promote timber production. The federal agencies concluded the locals needed recreational facilities too, so a lake was planned and in part sponsored by the US Navy, interested in creating an amphibious air craft base.

The Civilian Conservation Corps started construction of the lake in 1937, but the lake depth of fifty-five feet was dropped to thirty-five feet when it was discovered that a locally significant cemetery would be flooded. Upon completion in 1938, Holliday Lake was slated to be a "Total Recreation Area." The lake was made a state park in 1972 when campgrounds were added.

The orange-blazed Saunder's Creek Trail begins at Campground A and wanders down a stream toward the lake. Going right, and crossing the stream, the blue-blazed Lakeshore Nature Trail swings away from the shoreline and circles around a 4-H Camp that sits on the western bank of the lake. The interpretive trail for boaters follows the shore in this area unfrequented by hikers.

From the shore of the lake, hikers can see alders, cattails, and other shoreline plants. At about two miles, the trail crosses a bridge over the lake's dam. At 3.5 miles, a bridge spans Forbes Creek, and Holiday Creek is soon crossed. The creek illustrates a mystery about how the park was named. The creek is spelled with one "l," the state park with two—the reason why is unknown.

Both creeks are in the northern end of the lake, an area populated by beavers. The animals are particularly visible at dawn or dusk. The trail swings alongside Campground B and re-enters the beach area near picnic facilities. A trail in the beach area is yellow-blazed and can be followed around the point to the Saunder's Creek Trail and back to your car.

The park's developed facilities include a visitor center (with interpretive programs), campground (sixty sites, bathhouse), swimming beach (bathhouse,

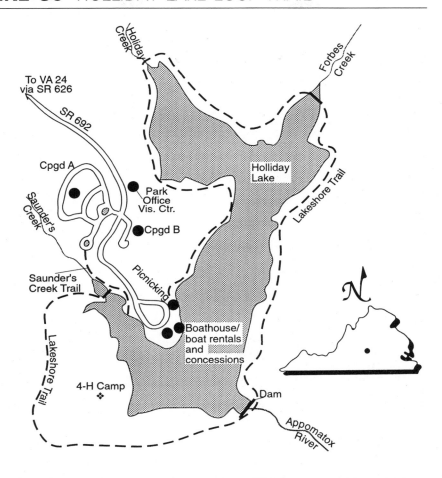

concession, store), and picnic area near the beach. Boating and fishing (state license required) are offered. There is a boat launch area, and canoes, paddleboats, sailboats, and rowboats are for rent during the season. A parking fee is charged, as are camping fees. Sites may be reserved in advance year-round for an additional fee by phone or mail from Virginia State Parks Reservation Center, P.O. Box 1895, Richmond, Virginia, 23215-1815, (800) 933-7275, 9 a.m.-4 p.m., Monday through Friday, with check, money order, Visa or MC.

# Twin Lakes State Park

Once called Prince Edward and Goodwin Lake State Park, Twin Lakes State Park has a "totally new management plan."

Over the years, Twin Lakes' mission has shifted to offering more recreational opportunities. This 270-acre park is only an hour from Richmond, and a pleasantly rolling, rural four-lane from the state capital, US 360, easily puts visitors in the mood to get out in the woods.

Like other Piedmont state parks, Twin Lakes is surrounded by state forest land. The Prince Edward-Gallion State Forest where hunting for deer, morial Day to Labor Day (camping, cabins, swimming, concessions). A modest conference facility, Cedar Crest Center, is located at the park.

Twin Lakes has two lakes, both circled by a trail with a connector between them. The Dogwood Hollow Nature Trail is the parks's easiest hike. The park's developed facilities include a campground (fifty-three sites, bathhouse), six cabins, and picnic areas for individual and group use. Boating and fishing (state license required) are offered. There are boat launch areas, and canoes, rowboats, and paddleboats are for rent during the season, Memorial Day to Labor Day (camping, cabins, swimming, concessions). A modest conference facility, Cedar Crest Center, is located at the park.

A parking fee is charged ($1.50), as are camping fees. Sites may be reserved in advance year-round for an additional fee by phone or mail from Virginia State Parks Reservation Center, P.O. Box 1895, Richmond, Virginia, 23215-1815, (800) 933-7275, 9 a.m.-4 p.m., Monday through Friday, with check, money order, Visa or MC.

**For more park information, contact: Twin Lakes State Park, Route 2, Box 70, Green Bay, VA 23942, (804) 392-3435.**

# HIKE 37 *TWIN LAKES STATE PARK LOOP HIKES*

**General description:** Two lakeshore loop hikes, with a connector, that permit easy to moderate walks of between one and four miles.
**Elevation gain and loss:** Negligible, but some short, steep pitches.
**Trailhead elevations:** Approximately 450 feet.
**Water availability:** Available in season at the park's developed facilities. In winter, water is available at the park ranger's office.
**Finding the trailhead:** Park in the day use area, south of the ranger office in the second parking area, near the swimming beach concessions. To find the park, see the directions under Dogwood Hollow Nature Trail.

**The hike:** A network of easy trails offer two lakeshore loops or a moderate circuit of both requiring only a little backtracking.

Goodwin Lake is the larger of the two, about forty acres, and the blue-blazed lakeshore trail makes the loop and follows the park road over the dam. The trail crosses a few bridges, passes a boat launch ramp, a nice place to start the hike, and totals 1.5 miles.

From the parking area at Goodwin Lake, the Between the Lakes Trail starts on the other side of the road and leads through the Between the Lakes Natural

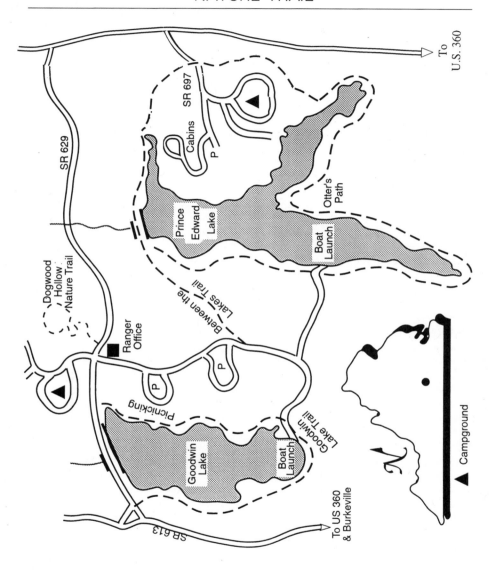

To U.S. 360

SR 697

Cabins

SR 629

Prince Edward Lake

Otter's Path

Boat Launch

Dogwood Hollow Nature Trail

Between the Lakes Trail

Ranger Office

Picnicking

Goodwin Lake

Goodwin Lake Trail

Boat Launch

SR 613

To US 360 & Burkeville

Campground

Area, an eighteen-acre area of shortleaf pine and various oaks. In this area of mature Piedmont forest, the hardwoods are slowly taking over the forest from the pioneering pines. The once-remote area was made accessible when the park's trails were rearranged in 1980's.

The yellow-blazed Between the Lakes Trail ends in .3 mile after intersecting the orange-blazed Otter's Path at the Prince Edward Lake dam. The four-mile Otter's Trail loops Prince Edward Lake, at times rising and falling rather steeply. the best railhead is the boat launch on the lake shore.

Despite its name, otters don't live along the trail, though beavers and muskrat do. You might also see evidence of other animals, among them deer, raccoons and foxes, both red and gray. Lakeshore sightings of turkeys, wood ducks, blue and green herons, several kinds of hawks, and owls are also possible. The endangered pileated woodpecker is also a resident.

The best bet for a longer hike that includes a taste of woodland walking is to follow the Between the Lakes Trail to and around Prince Edward Lake. The total hike is almost 4.5 miles. More energetic hikers should combine them both in a longer hike. Whichever lake you hike around first, the Between the Lakes Trail becomes a link that takes you to the other lake.

# HIKE 38     *DOGWOOD HOLLOW NATURE TRAIL*

**General description:** In 270-acre Twin Lakes State Park, just an hour from Richmond, there are four trails, one of which is an easy, mile-long, self-guiding interpretive loop, the Dogwood Hollow Trail.
**Elevation gain and loss:** Negligible.
**Trailhead elevation:** Approximately 450 feet.
**Water availability:** Water is available in season at the park's developed facilities. In winter, water is available at the ranger office.
**Finding the trailhead:** The park is 5 miles west of Burkeville on US 360. West of town, turn right on State Route 613, as directed by signs. Stay on 613 north 1.75 miles to a right turn on State Route 629 into the park. The trail starts .75 mile on the left after entering the park, opposite the park ranger's office, just beyond the Goodwin Lake dam.

**The hike:** The Dogwood Hollow Trail is the park's nature trail. A brochure is keyed to numbered posts on the path's one-mile loop. The blue-blazed trail starts in a parking area across State Route 629 from the park office, but it also connects to Campground A from the western side of the loop.

As with many nature trails, the path emphasizes the forest "community" and focuses on the area's transformation from farm to forest. In the area of Twin Lakes, the virgin forests gave way to farming through the mid-1800's. Erosion from that farming is obvious in places, as are trenches dug across the top of a dome-shaped earthen mound at the bottom of a hill. These are "robber trenches," the evidence left behind by people hoping to discover riches inside what they hoped was a Native American burial site.

# Pocahontas State Park and Richmond Area

Like Prince William Forest Park in Northern Virginia, Pocahontas State Park, just south of Richmond, sits slightly west of the Fall Line, the geographical point where the rolling forests of the Piedmont drop-off to the tidal influences of the coastal plain.

The 7,604-acre park was designated in 1934 by the Department of the Interior and christened as the Swift Creek Recreational Demonstration Area. The park, planned all along to be later managed by the state of Virginia, got under way in 1935 with a Civilian Conservation Corps camp. The CCC-built lakes and a number of buildings from that period, including the park's visitor center are still in use.

The park became Pocahontas State Park in 1946. Like many state parks, Pocahontas is surrounded by state forest land, but unlike others, the park holds the deed to the forest land, instead of the reverse. That gives priority to recreation, and in recent years a new master plan, funded by the state and Chesterfield County, is creating expanded facilities to better serve the large urban populations that lie within twenty miles.

The trail network at the park has been improved in the last few years, and new trails are planned. Besides the seven developed trails that exist, which include a five-mile bicycle path and a paved handicapped trail, many miles of other paths wander through the forest.

The evidence of timber harvesting is visible in Pocahontas, including loblolly pine plantations that are visible on the bicycle path. Today, the park is managed more for aesthetics. Large tracts of forest provide fine trailless hiking opportunities for people proficient with map and compass.

The park's hiking trails focus on the two largest lakes, 150-acre Swift Creek Lake, and Beaver Lake, which is sometimes called Third Branch Lake. Both lakes have seen better days. Development west of Pocahontas is slowly silting the lakes, causing both to grow shallower. Increased nutrients have led to plant growth and algae blooms, particularly in Beaver Lake, which in many places is only a foot or two deep. In effect, Beaver Lake is becoming a freshwater marsh.

All of that resulted in the termination of swimming in Swift Creek Lake in 1981, the year the park opened a massive swimming pool complex. With over 17,500 square feet of swimming area, it is reputed to be the largest in the state (open Memorial Day weekend through Labor Day weekend). During that same season, rowboats and paddleboats are available for rent and fishing is permitted with a state license.

The park has a campground (fifty-four sites, bathhouse). Group camping facilities are impressive, with campsites and group cabin facilities for sixteen to 112 people, and dining halls. The visitor center offers an extensive list of programs, including boat tours, presentations, hikes, and environmental education.

A parking fee is charged, as are camping fees. Sites may be reserved in advance year-round for an additional fee by phone or mail from Virginia State Parks Reservation Center, P.O. Box 1895, Richmond, Virginia, 23215-1815, (800) 933-7275, 9 a.m.-4 p.m., Monday through Friday, with check, money order, Visa or MC.

**For more park information, call: Pocahontas State Park, 10300 State Park Road, Chesterfield, VA 23832, (804) 796-4255.**

# HIKE 39 *BEAVER LAKE AND POWHATAN TRAIL HIKES*

**General description:** The Beaver Lake Trail (2.5-mile loop) and the Powhatan Trail (2.3-mile loop) are easy to moderate hikes in Pocahontas State Park.
**Elevation gain and loss:** 100 feet or less, with gradual grades.
**Trailhead elevation:** Trailheads range from approximately 150 to 250 feet.
**Water availability:** In season, water is available at the park's developed facilities. In winter, water is available just past the visitor center at the year-round restrooms in the parking lot for the picnic area and pool.
**Finding the trailheads:** The park is located twenty miles south of Richmond. Take I-95 south, and get off at exit 6. Go west on State Route 10 to State Route 655, Beach Road. The park is well marked. To reach the Beaver Lake Trail, go straight after entering the park, cross Swift Creek, and turn left into the visitor center parking lot. To reach the Powhatan Trail, enter the park and go straight toward the visitor center. Enter the first picnic area on the right.

**The hikes:** Beaver Lake is the smallest of the park's two lakes, and the one most affected by siltation and a gradual transformation to marshland (see the entry for Pocahontas State Park).

The lake is nevertheless scenic and the center of a bottomland hardwood forest of species such as oak, sycamore, birch, ash, maple, yellow poplar, and sweetgum. These forests, especially where they lie beside wetland ecosystems, as they do on the western side of Beaver Lake, are considered to be among the park's most sensitive and unique natural areas. Managers strive to preserve these areas, and the recreational emphasis of the lands surrounding Beaver Lake is evidence of that.

The trail leaves the visitor center combined with the Ground Pine Nature Trail. After descending west along the lakeshore for .25 mile, the Ground Pine Path goes right and the Beaver Lake Trail continues with the lakeshore. The trail follows the side of the lake, situated at 140 feet above sea level, and then the stream that feeds it. The trail passes through groves of large trees, with views of the lake, and possibly beavers.

At about 1.5 miles, the trail reaches the site of an old gristmill. Like others located every fifteen or twenty miles throughout the surrounding countryside, the mill was built in the mid-1800's and served the immediate region around it. The white-blazed Third Branch Trail branches right, a .3-mile connector to the green-blazed Old Mill Bicycle Trail, a five-mile loop that leads bicyclists on a larger circle around Beaver Lake.

The Beaver Lake Trail crosses the stream and continues to the dam, spillway, and bridge across the outlet brook at 2.3 miles. From there, hikers reach the visitor center on the paved, handicapped-accessible Awareness Walk (red-blazed, less than .5 mile). The return to the visitor center makes the hike about three miles.

The Powhatan Trail, a red/white-blazed former horse trail, follows a ridge from the first picnic area, about 275 feet above sea level. The trail then branches into one large and one small loop near the shore of Swift Creek Lake. The lowest of the loops dips to about 135 feet. From that elevation, it's possible to bushwhack to Swift Creek Lake (at 120 feet above sea level), but the trail

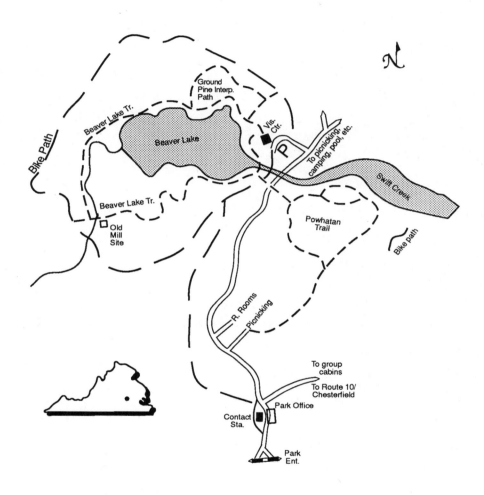

*Hikers descend to the spillway view at Pocahontas State Park.*

doesn't reach the lakeshore. The elevation changes offer a little exercise, but the trail isnt difficult. Near the lake, a new connector links with the Beaver Lake Trail.

The fire road-width Powhatan Trail runs to the lake through a mature hardwood forest punctuated by the shiny shapes of American holly trees. Deer, turkey, and piliated woodpeckers are among the residents. The first part of the trail and the largest loop is two miles. The shorter, distant-most loop adds another .3 mile.

# HIKE 40 *POCAHONTAS STATE PARK, THE GROUND PINE PATH NATURE TRAIL*

**General description:** Pocahontas State Park, a 7,604-acre park near Richmond has seven trails, including a five-mile bicycle trail, a paved handicapped trail (The Awareness Walk), and the Ground Pine Path, a nature trail keyed to a numbered brochure.
**Elevation gain and loss:** Fifty feet, with gradual grades.
**Trailhead elevation:** 200 feet.
**Water availability:** In season, water is available at the park's developed facilities. In winter, water is available just past the visitor center at the year-round restrooms in the parking lot for the picnic area and pool.
**Finding the trailhead:** The park is located twenty miles south of Richmond. Take Interstate 95 south, and get off at exit 6. Go west on State Route 10 to State Route 655, Beach Road. The park is well marked. After entering the park, go straight, cross Swift Creek, and turn left into the visitor center parking area.

**The hike:** The Ground Pine Path Nature Trail is a one-mile nature loop that explores rolling terrain and the shoreline of Beaver Lake. A brochure is keyed to numbered posts on the trail.

The trail's general theme of plant and animal interdependence is nicely complemented by line drawings of plants that hikers can easily see along the way. The shallow lake is dotted with water lilies, and at post five, a natural spring leaks from the ground. Lengthy muscadine grape vines reach from the ground to the sunny treetops, and in the understory, American holly, dogwood, and ground pine or running cedar thrive in the shade. Farther on, oaks, beeches, and tulip poplars cluster in hardwood groves. The trail circles back to its start near the visitor center.

# HIKE 41 *NEW KENT NATURE TRAIL*

**General description:** A three-loop, 2.5-mile interpretive nature trail of high scenic and educational value.
**Elevation gain and loss:** Negligible.
**Trailhead elevation:** Forty feet.
**Water availability:** Streams are not suitable for drinking.
**Finding the trailhead:** Parking area on eastbound side of US 33 east of Richmond, about three miles from US 33 exit on I-64, and one half mile east of the US 33 junction with VA 249 and VA 30.
**For more information, contact:** Chesapeake Forest Products Company, Woodlands Division, Box 311, West Point, VA 23181, 804-843-5402.

**The hike:** This trail is one of the finest free, public use trails on private land in the state of Virginia.

The trail, owned and maintained by the Chesapeake Forest Products Company of nearby West Point, Virginia, offers a scenic respite from urban areas such as Richmond, Petersburg, and Hampton. The trail wanders along

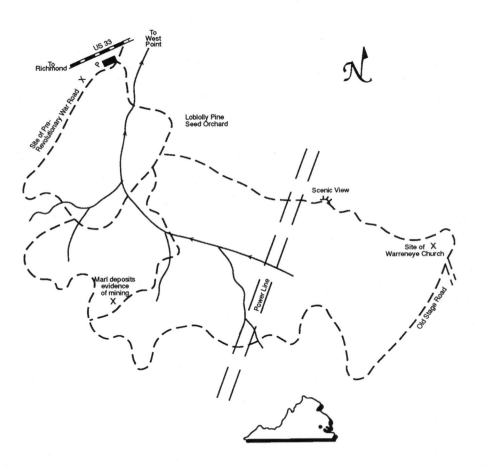

and dips into stream valleys in a wooded landscape typical of the Virginia Tidewater. Trees you'll notice on the trail include yellow poplar, sycamore, sweet gum (with its telltale spiny gumballs), beech, red maple, dogwood, eastern red cedar, American holly, and various oaks.

The trail is mostly gradual, with few steep sections and only short climbs. If all three loops are walked, the trip can take more than three hours and be moderately strenuous. With leaves on the ground, some sidehill portions of the trail can be tricky.

The trail loops are marked with numbered posts keyed to a highly informative booklet printed on brown paper bag-type paper manufactured by the Chesapeake Company's West Point paper plant. The trail and booklet are a fine resource for families, schools, and scout groups. The Chesapeake Company asks groups of ten or more to call ahead to insure finding sufficient brochures at the trailhead dispenser.

The posted points of interest range from identified plant species to evidence of historic use of the area by man. A number of the posts mark places where the concepts of ecology and forestry stand out. Needless to say, timber harvesting techniques such as clearcutting are explained and supported by the paper company brochure. The booklet focuses on loblolly pine, the primary type of tree planted on the company's timberlands, which is visible at one prominent site on the trail where the trees stand in neat rows. The booklet supports clearcutting, using the example of "clearcut wildlife openings," while omitting a clear statement that the practice is controversial, especially in diverse forests such as the eastern hardwood ecosystems of the Southern Appalachians. The booklet may therefore be a bit one-sided. Nevertheless, the educational impact of the trail is impressive and largely impartial.

Easy, moderate, and more strenuous options are created by the three-loop trail design. The intelligent layout snakes through the forest, making the most of the available area and allowing hikers to feel like they're in a forest of considerable size.

Points of interest along the trail include a pre-Revolutionary stage road that ran from Plum Point on the York River, the start of a ferry to the town of West Point, to a road that linked Williamsburg and New Kent County Courthouse. The trail follows the road, and then veers away offering a detour on a colonial highway, now quiet and leaf covered. Nearby is the site of the Warreneye Church, built in 1703, and now marked only by elaborately worded gravestones honoring a young doctor and a sea captain.

The trail also contains evidence of mining for deposits of marl, mixtures of calcium and magnesium spread on fields as a fertilizer.

# Prince William Forest Park

This 17,000-acre National Park Service preserve is the largest remaining natural area in the megalopolis of northern Virginia. It is also the largest such forest in the National Park Service System. That makes Prince William Forest Park a magnet for hikers, with thirty-five miles of paths that wander between the Piedmont and the coastal plain in the area south of Woodbridge and north of the Quantico U.S. Marine Corps Reservation.

Prince William Forest Park is easily reached from Interstate 95 south of Woodbridge. The Quantico/Triangle exit is within sight of the park entrance.

Once heavily farmed and even mined, the area has gradually returned to woods much like those that Captain John Smith probably saw when he wandered away from the Potomac River after landing in the vicinity of nearby Dumfries in the early 1600s. Today the park is popular and has extensively developed facilities for camping. There are campgrounds for tents and recreational vehicles, and organized groups have tent campgrounds and cabin camps. Those cabins, like many of the park's facilities, were built by the Civilian Conservation Corps.

The park's other possibilities include fishing in lakes (Virginia license required), bicycling (on the Park Central Drive scenic loop road and fireroads, but not trails), and picnicking (at two separate areas, one with a shelter available by reservation). A visitor center is open all year (closed December 25 and January 1), and visitors can find interpretive exhibits, information services, and educational programs there. An environmental education center is being created at a former nature center in the park. Bird watching and animal observation are popular. Park naturalists schedule guided hikes and activities all year, many of them oriented around area wildlife including wild turkeys, beaver, and deer. (Pets must be on a leash at all times, and in some cases they are prohibited.)

The park's ten major trails wind past streams, drainages, ridges, and lakes. Hikes range from very short to loops of up to twenty miles. Length is generally the best measure of hiking difficulty in the park, though some trails have short, steep climbs and parts of the park are surprisingly hilly. Four nature trails in the park are self-guided with signs or brochures to inform hikers. Trail junctions in the park are marked with mileage posts.

No backpack camping is allowed on the trails, except in a 400-acre backpack camping area called the Chopawamsic Backcountry. The Chopawamsic is separated from the main park and surrounded by the Quantico Marine Corps Reservation. The backpack area is closed during hunting season, from October 15 to February 1 (no hunting is allowed in the park). Camping in the Chopawamsic requires a permit, and campers are limited to ten privatized sites, each reached by a .25-mile spur trail from the main loop trail that circles the area. No pets are permitted.

There are seasonal considerations. Manmade structures at the pyrite mine site, the highlight of one hike in this book, are most visible in the winter, and ticks, a problem at the height of summer, are a thing of the past then. Also in winter, the park's wide, gradual trails can be nice for cross-country skiing when snow conditions cooperate.

The park's future may hold surprises. Prince William's management plan, in the works for ten years, was released in 1992. That document could spark changes in the relationship between the park and the large Marine Corps Reservation. Land trades are being considered that could swap the Chopawamsic for a backcountry addition ten times its current size. That might provide the unusual opportunity to reroute VA 619 around the larger area, expanding the park's status as a contiguous forest.

**For more information, including a reasonable trail map, contact: Superintendent, Prince William Forest Park, 18100 Park Headquarters Road, Triangle, Virginia, 22172; or call the Visitor Center, 703-221-7181.**

# HIKES 42, 43, 44

## PYRITE MINE TRAIL, PRINCE WILLIAM FOREST PARK LOOP FARMS TO FOREST TRAIL

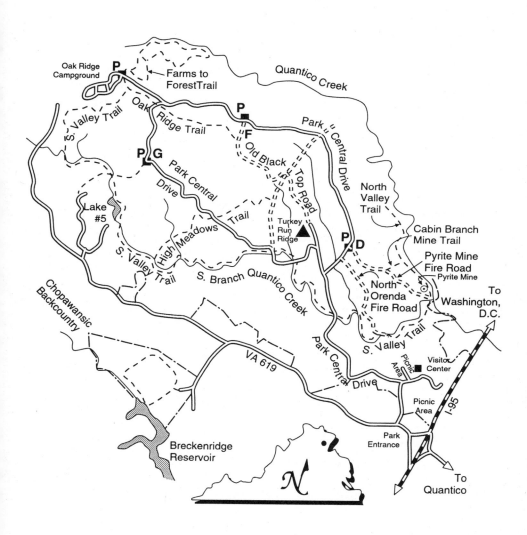

# HIKE 42 *PYRITE MINE LOOP HIKE*

**General description:** This is a moderate and scenic three-mile loop hike focusing on the remains of a Pyrite Mine that operated in the Prince William Forest Park around the turn of the century.

**Elevation gain and loss:** 340 feet.

**Trailhead elevation:** 220 feet.

**Low point:** Eighty feet.

**Water availability:** Water is available at the picnic area and visitor center on the way into park.

**Finding the trailhead:** Park in the first parking area, Parking Lot D, on the one-way, right hand branch of Park Central Drive scenic loop. The parking area is on the left, between the North Orenda Fire Road and Pyrite Mine Fire Road.

**The hike:** This loop features a variety of terrain, which includes mature forest and streamside hiking and provides an interesting insight into early human uses of the park.

From the late 1800's to the early 20th century, the Cabin Branch Mine employed as many as 300 people extracting pyrite from a number of deep mine shafts. A virtual village of miners clustered around the mine processing the pyrite, commonly called fool's gold, and valuable as a source of sulphur.

The mine was particularly profitable during World War I when pyrite was used to produce gunpowder. After the war, the mine's profitability plummeted, and it closed when workers went on strike. Soon thereafter, Civilian Conservation Corps camps were built in the park, and the CCC workers dismantled the mine site using many of the materials in other park projects. By the time the CCC was finished constructing bridges, lakes, and cabin camps, the mine site was little more than the prominent remains of foundations. Today, those ruins are best recognized in the winter.

The hike starts on the Pyrite Mine Fire Road, a dirt-surfaced lane occasionally used for motor access by rangers. After .5 mile, take the Cabin Branch Mine Trail to the left, a steep .4-mile drop to Quantico Creek and the North Valley Trail.

Going right on the North Valley Trail, hikers reach the mine site in a little more than .1 mile. The trail winds through the prominent remains of buildings such as the block house, crusher house, and conveyor belt assembly. Not far beyond the mine, the Pyrite Mine Fire Road comes in from the right.

Stay left at that junction and follow the South Valley Trail up the South Branch of Quantico Creek. This is the junction between the rolling hills of the Piedmont and the lower coastal plain of the Tidewater. The streamside outcroppings signal the fall line, the drop between the two geographical regions of Virginia.

A .9 mile hike on the South Valley Trail brings you to the junction with the North Orenda Fire Road. When combined with the gradual rise of the stream, this fire road creates an easy ascent, one mile back to your car on the Park Central Drive.

This is a more pleasant hike than the Pyrite Mine Fire Road. The North Orenda Fire Road is not used by vehicles, so the surface is mossy and grassy.

Trees, some of them quite large, touch over the trail, creating a more primitive atmosphere. The recommended direction of this hike is the easy way. In the opposite direction, hikers climb the steepness of the Cabin Branch Mine Trail.

# HIKE 43 *PRINCE WILLIAM FOREST PARK LOOP*

**General description:** An approximately nine-mile, moderately strenuous loop from the Oak Ridge Campground down through the center of the park and back up the South Branch of Quantico Creek past Lake #5.
**Elevation gain and loss:** 540 feet.
**Trailhead elevation:** 370 feet.
**Low point:** 100 feet.
**Water availability:** Fountains and restrooms available in season at the trailhead in Oak Ridge Campground.
**Finding the trailhead:** The trail starts at a signed (South Valley Trail) parking area on the Oak Ridge Campground access road, a facility reached approximately six miles from the park entrance via the two-way left fork of the Park Central Drive, a scenic loop road.

**The hike:** This energetic amble takes in virtually every kind of ecosystem and scenery in the park.

Starting from the trailhead, bear left on the new Oak Ridge Trail and in .5 mile cross the Park Central Drive. On the other side of the road, the trail is flanked with ground cedar. Continue for a 1.2-mile stretch to the Old Black Top Forest Road. At the beginning of this road, a .2-mile trail splits to the left to Parking Lot F, another possible starting point.

Follow the Old Black Top Road, which is not paved. You pass through mature oak and pine forest on the .7-mile walk to the junction with the Taylor Farm Road. At the junction, a motor access road goes left, so turn right on the dirt-surfaced Taylor Farm Road.

In .3 mile, you'll reach the junction with the High Meadows Trail. The site of the Taylor farm is here and includes an old cemetery. This is also one of the better places in the park to pick up a hitchhiking tick in the summer, so watch where you walk.

Bearing left and continuing on the Taylor Farm Road, the trail drops and in .6 mile reaches the South Valley Trail. Turn right onto the South Valley Trail, and after crossing the Park Central Drive, this starts a more than three-mile meander beside the South Branch of Quantico Creek and Lake #5.

Notice the large rock outcroppings typical of the fall line, along this stretch of trail. Once granite, this rock has been pressure-treated by nature to become gneiss. In 1.9 miles, the High Meadows Trail comes in on the right. The forest here is a dramatic change from the heavily logged and farmed landscape of a century ago. No longer does silt wash down the creek to the Potomac. The stabilization of this watershed contributes to the improving quality of water downstream in the mighty Potomac.

Further upstream on the South Valley Trail, before reaching Lake #5, you'll cross a new bridge. This surprising, double ellipse truss bridge is a design of Sir Isaac Newton.

Past the lake, and 1.5 miles from the High Meadows Trail, you'll reach the junction of the Mawavi Fire Road. To the right, Parking Lot G is only .4 mile away on the Park Central Drive, another good starting point.

Continuing on, the South Valley Trail follows the creek, then veers off, climbing and winding to Oak Ridge Campground and the parking area, 2.3 miles from the Mawavi Fire Road.

# HIKE 44 *FARMS TO FOREST TRAIL*

**General description:** A 1.1-mile, easy interpretive trail, and a 2.5-mile extension that may be the best place in Prince William Forest Park to see beaver.
**Elevation gain and loss:** Negligible on interpretive loop, 280 feet on longer loop.
**Trailhead elevation:** Approximately 370 feet.
**Lowpoint:** 230 feet.
**Water availability:** Fountains and restrooms in season at trailhead in Oak Ridge Campground.
**Finding the trailhead:** The trail starts at a signed (South Valley Trail) parking area on the Oak Ridge Campground access road, a facility reached approximately six miles from the park entrance via the left fork of the Park Central Drive, a scenic loop road.

**The hike:** The 1.1-mile interpretive loop emphasizes the long history of human habitation in the park and the decades-long return to forest. By the early 1700s, the Quantico Creek watershed had been cleared for tobacco cultivation, a cash crop shipped out of the nearby deep-water harbor at Dumfries.

That all ended when erosion stripped the depleted topsoil from the farms, disastrously dumping so much silt into the Dumfries harbor that it became a marsh. The economy rebounded a little with the early 1900s mining of pyrite in the park (see Pyrite Mine Loop), but by 1930, when the Park Service received the land, mining and farming were finished and the land was ripe for the reclamation efforts of the new Civilian Conservation Corps.

Starting on the trail, hikers can go left or right on the first loop. Stands of tall pines on the trail's first loop are the remains of old farm fields. The trail brochure focuses on this progress from pioneering pines to the mature hardwood forest, principally oak, found elsewhere in the park. A colonial road is visible on this section of trail.

The second loop of the trail is actually unrelated to the interpretive path. The longer trail wanders for 1.7 miles, making a total hike of 2.8 miles possible.

The larger loop is the park's best location for seeing beaver activity. Centuries ago, beaver trapping was intense here, the result of European demand for beaver coats and hats. By the mid-1800s, the animal had vanished from the area of Prince William Park. Since being reintroduced in the 1950s, beavers have made a comeback. Their woodland dams trap silt, enriching the forest when the beavers move on. (The Mary Bird Branch Trail, accessible from parking lot E and the Turkey Run Ridge Environmental Center, is another park trail where beaver activity is very visible.)

The trail passes through heavier forest on the longer loop, and passes beaver impoundments on its descent along a tributary of Quantico Creek. The last .5 mile is a steep descent of about 140 feet, a drop one must ascend on the way out.

# Mason Neck State Park

# HIKE 45 *MASON NECK STATE PARK AND HIKING TRAILS*

**General description:** An increasingly popular state park with three miles of trails that reach one of the state's best wetland waterfowl viewing areas.
**Elevation gain and loss:** Minimal.
**Trailhead elevation:** Ten feet.
**Water availability:** Water is available in season at the park's developed facilities. In winter, water is available at the year-round restrooms in the picnic area.
**Finding the trailhead:** The park is about twenty miles from Washington D.C. in the southeast corner of Fairfax County. Access is via U.S. 1, reached from the northbound lanes of I-95 on exit 161, and from the southbound lanes on exit 163 (Lorton). After exiting from the north, those taking exit 163 should go under the railroad trestle to a right turn on Armistead Road. Then take a right at the first traffic light onto U.S. 1. Turn on State Route 242, Gunston Hall Road, and in just over five miles turn right onto High Point Road at the Mason Neck Management Area sign. The park's contact station is then about two miles, and the visitor center trailhead is about 2.5 miles beyond that.
**For more park information:** Mason Neck State Park, 7301 High Point Road, Lorton, Virginia 22079, (703) 550-0960.

**The hike:** Mason Neck State Park is one of a number of parks, including a national wildlife refuge, that preserve the natural environment of Mason Neck. The historic peninsula juts out into the Potomac, and encircles Belmont Bay, to the south, and Pohick Bay, to the north. The area gains its name from George Mason, whose home, Gunston Hall, is a popular attraction for visitors.

Mason Neck, like other parts of the fast-growing Fairfax County area, could very well have become a highly developed area with little attention given to the natural environment. But two bald eagle nests were discovered in 1965, and conservationists awoke to the fact that the peninsula's prominent wetlands were an essential habitat for many migrating waterfowl.

In ensuing years, a beltway road, a natural gas pipeline, an airport, and a landfill were all proposed for the sensitive area. All those plans were dropped, and now a state park and national wildlife refuge are among lands preserved as part of the Mason Neck Cooperative Management Area.

The 1,804-acre park sits on the southeast shore of Belmont Bay. The site is an active heron rookery, and attracts bald eagles, whistling swans, and many species of ducks. Over 220 species of birds and waterfowl have been recorded here.

Three miles of trails facilitate the study of that rich environment, as do an extensive visitor center and environmental education center. The visitor center (open daily during the summer, weekends April/May and September/October) features exhibits on the area's wildlife, the history of the Mason Neck, and efforts to preserve the Cooperative Management Area.

The park is also one of seven Chesapeake Bay area state parks that offer

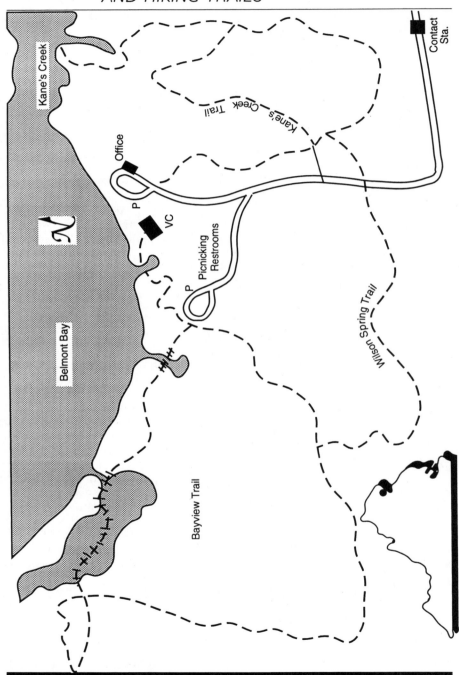

planned curriculum options for K-12 teachers interested in teaching about the environment. That program is based in the park's environmental education center, which contains a wet lab, research materials, and sampling equipment. The park's staff routinely helps plan visits and use of the facilities. A wide variety of interpretive programs and a picnic area are also available. A parking fee is charged.

Don't forget your binoculars when you visit this park. Mason Neck State Park's three miles of trails offer some of the state's best opportunities for viewing waterfowl.

The park has three trails; two loops and a connector. Both the Kane's Creek Trail, and the Bay View Trail, at about a mile each, are easy loops with developed viewing areas. Luckily the more avid hiker can link the two, creating a moderate three-mile day hike that will have wildlife watchers grinning from ear to ear.

Both Kane's Creek and Bay View Trail loops can be started separately at the visitor center. The best bet is to park there, and loop the entire trail system.

Take the red-blazed Bay View Trail from the visitor center, to the picnic area, and go right at the fork. This part of the path follows near the shoreline, crossing boardwalks through wetland areas. At the trail's most distant loop, two observation benches provide views of the tidal marsh.

Swinging south away from the shore, take the right turn onto the yellow-blazed Wilson Spring Trail. You'll cross the park entrance road and intersect the blue-blazed Kane's Creek Trail. Take a right at the junction, then bear right at the next junction on a spur to reach an observation blind. The viewpoint perches on a ridge between two fingers of Kane's Creek.

Retracing your steps, take the first right to continue on the Kane's Creek loop. Take the next right after that (at the close of the loop), and that spur takes you back to the visitor center and your car.

---

# Northern Virginia Regional Park Authority Trails

# HIKE 46 *THE BLUE TRAIL*

**General description:** A variety of trails managed by the innovative Northern Virginia Regional Park Authority. Hikes include an eighteen-mile route along Bull Run and Occoquan River, an easy wildflower walk, scenic loop hikes near the Potomac, and a forty-five-mile rails to trails urban greenway path.
**Elevation gain and loss:** Neglible, except on the Blue Trail, an eighteen-mile riverside hike.
**Finding the trailheads:** See individual hikes.
**For more information:** The Northern Virginia Regional Park Authority, 5400 Ox Road, Fairfax Station, VA 22039, (703) 352-5900.
**The Park Authority:** This organization of northern Virginia counties and cities has led the way in creating an exemplary network of parks and recreation sites for metropolitan residents. The nationally noteworthy system warrants visitation by hikers from outside the region.

The authority got its start in the late 1950s when the Northern Virginia Planning District Commission recommended creating a multi-jurisdictional agency to preserve open space. Citizens already engaged in that effort legislatively organized as the Northern Virginia Regional Park Authority in 1959. Today, the authority combines the counties of Arlington, Fairfax, and Loudon, with the cities of Alexandria, Fairfax, and Falls Church.

The efforts of the authority have netted more than 9,000 acres of preserved parkland. The range of recreation available is nationally noteworthy. Cabins, conference facilities, swimming pools, regular and miniature golf courses, skeet, trap and archery areas, fishing, boating, camping, and picnicing are just the beginning. Playing fields exist, and various kinds of equipment are on hand for many different competitve team sports.

And then there are hiking trails. These range from the seventy-five-acre Meadowlark Gardens botanical park, with more than four miles of trails, to the eighteen-mile Blue Trail that links five regional parks in the Bull Run-Occoquan River drainage.

Entrance fees are charged at some parks for out-of-region residents. Alcoholic beverages are prohibitied in parks (except at certain places and times), and pets must be leashed. Most parks are open year-round, and hunting is prohibited.

The park authority offers a variety of publications and brochures about individual parks, and hikers are encouraged to contact the agency for greater details. The options are too broad to be completely covered here.

## *The Blue Trail (or Bull Run-Occoquan Trail)*

This eighteen-mile, blue-blazed route is an end to end or out and back riverside path that parallels Bull Run in the west and the Occoquan River farther east. The trail is accessible at Bull Run Regional Park, Hemlock Overlook, Bull Run Marina, and Fountainhead Regional Park, all part of 5,000 acres of forest and marshland that shelter diverse bird and animal life. Plans call for the trail to be extended to Sandy Run Regional Park.

The elevation of this moderate trail ranges between 150 and 250 feet above sea level. Much of the trail is level or gradual, with even substantial elevation changes usually less than seventy-five vertical feet.

The eight-mile section between Bull Run and Hemlock Overlook Regional Parks is a nice place to try the trail. The trail is mostly level to the Centreville Road, and from there the trail undulates over a variety of terrain, and passes Civil War breastworks. Near aptly named Hemlock Overlook, the trail is lined by mature hemlock trees. An out and back from either park is easy to moderately strenuous depending on distance. The total eight miles between parks takes three to four hours.

Trail sections from Hemlock Overlook to Bull Run Marina, and from Bull Run Marina to Fountainhead, are about four and six miles respectively. To reach Bull Run Regional Park, exit westbound from I-66 at exit 52, Centreville. Go right, south on U.S. 29 two miles to a left turn onto Bull Run Post Office Road. Take a right onto Bull Run Drive and reach the park entrance.

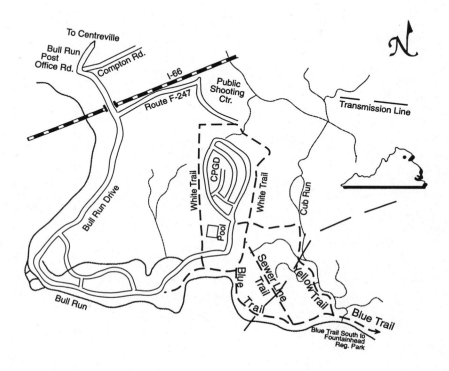

*The Potomac passes serenely beneath Red Rock Wilderness Overlook Regional Park in Northern Virginia.* Northern Virginia Regional Park Authority photo.

# Westmoreland State Park and Hiking Trails

# HIKE 47 BIG MEADOWS INTERPRETIVE TRAIL, TURKEY NECK TRAIL

**General description:** This 1,299-acre state park, flanked by the birthplace of George Washington and Robert E. Lee's early home, is situated on scenic cliffs above the Potomac River. There are seven trails, including a .5-mile interpretive trail, and a 2.5-mile hike that explores Coastal Plain wetlands.
**Elevation gain and loss:** Negligible.
**Trailhead elevation:** Less than thirty feet.
**Water availability:** Water is available in season at the park's developed facilities. In winter, water is available at the ranger office.
**Finding the trailheads:** The park is about seventy miles northeast of Richmond. From either U.S. 360 or U.S. 301, the nearest major roads, take VA 3 to the vicinity of Montross. Five miles northwest of Montross, take VA 347 north to the park. Trailhead locations are described for each hike.
**For more park information:** Westmoreland State Park, Rt. 1, Box 600, Montross, VA 22520, (804) 493-8821.

**The hike:** Westmoreland is best known for its extensive summer (Memorial Day through Labor Day) recreational activities, among them swimming at a pool complex (bathhouse, concession area), saltwater fishing and boating (paddle boats/row boats for rent, boat ramp, supplies), picnicking, and camping (118 sites, twenty group, bathhouse, groceries).

The park has twenty-four rental cabins and a nice restaurant that overlooks a spectacular river view from Horsehead Cliffs. The restaurant, and many of the trails and other facilities were built by the Civilian Conservation Corps. This is one of Virginia's original six state parks.

Hikers will find the trails a wealth of insight into the unique setting of the Coastal Plain. Just walking the beach is fascinating. The park's visitor center contains an exhibit of shark's teeth and other fossils taken from the rich sediments that make up the cliffs. The fossils on the beach are protected, but visitors can look.

The area's geology is intriguing, and a walk on the shore, and tour of the visitor center, is a worthwhile way to explore it. The center offers guided walks and summer interpretive programs. Westmoreland is one of seven Chesapeake Bay state parks that offer an environmental education curriculum for use by teachers.

A parking fee is charged, as are camping fees. Sites may be reserved in advance year-round for an additional fee by phone or mail from Virginia State Parks Reservation Center, P.O. Box 1895, Richmond, Virginia, 23215-1815, (800) 933-7275, 9 a.m.-4 p.m., Monday through Friday, with check, money order, Visa or MC.

The park's trails, seven in all, primarily serve to transport guests between developed facilities. However, the Big Meadows Interpretive Trail and the Turkey Neck Trail combine to form a loop hike through scenic wetlands, with striking views of Horsehead Cliffs and the Potomac River.

The red-blazed Big Meadows Interpretive Trail begins near the park's

*Horsehead Cliffs rise above the Potomac from this view in Westmoreland State Park.*

easternmost collection of cabins. The trail starts just beyond the visitor center, on the right side of a split in the road on the way to the cabins. A grassy parking area on the right, and a sign, mark the start of the .6-mile trail.

A brochure is keyed to the path's eleven interpretive stations, most designed to inspire hikers to imagine what it must have been like before the settlers when Powhatan Indians roamed the area. At stop eight, a left turn takes hikers to the beach and a nice view of the cliffs and river. The Potomac, at this point only thirty miles from the Chesapeake Bay, contains salt water and fluctuates with the tides.

Bearing right at stop eight, the trail crosses a bridge and reaches an observation tower at the juncture of Big Meadows Swamp and Yellow Swamp. The trail connects from there to the main loop of the blue-blazed Turkey Neck Trail, an approximately 1.5-mile loop that skirts the swamp, crosses bridges and a boardwalk beside Yellow Swamp, and returns to the junction with the interpretive trail. The total loop is about 2.5 miles. The loop itself is bisected by the Beaver Dam Trail (.4 mile).

Hikers could also not make the loop, but continue to the left where a spur of the Turkey Neck Trail branches off toward the park entrance. Along this trail, a spur goes left to the campground, continuing right goes to a parking spot on the main park road. Following the road to the right leads past the campground entrance and the visitor center for a round-trip of about 3.5 miles.

Trails west of the park's main road can be sampled from the trailhead for the Laurel Point Trail. The gravel parking area and sign is opposite Campground C, and just south of Campground B on the right as you're leaving the park.

The 1.3-mile, orange-blazed Laurel Point Trail runs through previously farmed land. Evidence of fencing and gates is visible to observant hikers. The path passes Rock Spring Pond at about .5 mile, on the left, and Rock Spring Pond Trail, on the right. Rock Spring Pond is a small reservoir built by the Civilian Conservation Corps. The .5-mile Rock Spring Pond Trail, blazed green, leads from the dam of the pond to the park road, just north of campground A, on the right as you're leaving the park.

Continuing on the Laurel Point Trail, the path terminates at the boat ramp and rental area in just under two miles. Hikers can walk the road back to their car, or take the yellow-blazed Beach Trail from the pool area, a .5-mile ascending hike to a trailhead near the camp store. From there, a roadside walk to the car yields a hike of just over three miles.

*An observation tower gives wildlife watchers a nice view of Big Meadows Swamp in Westmoreland State Park.*

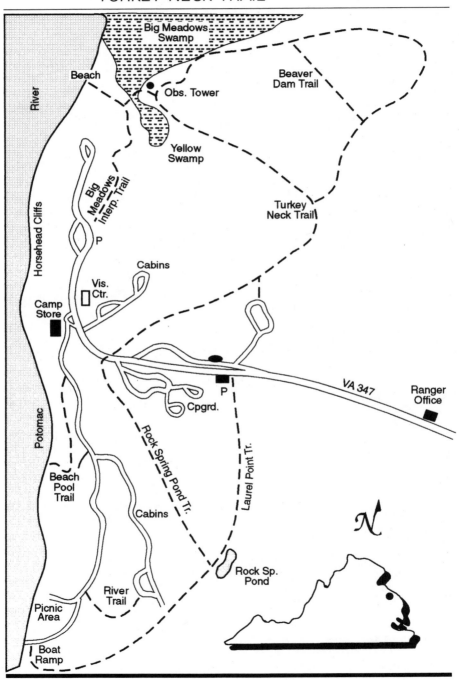

Hikers can also turn right from the road on the Rock Spring Pond Trail, reach the pond in .5 mile, turn left on the Laurel Point Trail, and return to their car. That total circuit is about four miles.

# Newport News

# HIKE 48  *THE NOLAND TRAIL*

**General description:** A noteworthy new five-mile trail that can be hiked in easy, two- and three-mile segments. The path winds around Lake Maury, on the grounds of the Mariner's Museum in Newport News.
**Elevation gain and loss:** Minimal.
**Trailhead elevation:** Less than fifty feet.
**Water availability:** The Mariner's Museum parking area is the start for the trail. The noted maritime museum is open year-round (9 a.m.-5 p.m. except noon-5 p.m. Sundays, closed Christmas) and water can be acquired there. In season, a water fountain is located at the Williams Field picnic area, about 2.2 miles from the museum.
**Finding the trailhead:** The Mariner's Museum is located at the intersection of J. Clyde Morris and Warwick boulevards in Newport News. From I-64, take exit 62 and go southwest on U.S. 17 to reach the museum.
**For further information:** The Mariner's Museum, 100 Museum Drive, Newport News, VA 23606-3759, (804) 595-0368.

**The hike:** The Noland Trail is one of the state's best examples of a privately owned trail that is free to the public. The Mariner's Museum, a nationally significant collection of artifacts and exhibits chronicling Eastern America's seafaring heritage, is situated on a 550-acre tract surrounding Lake Maury. The 167-acre impoundment is named after Matthew Fontaine Maury, Virginia native son and historic oceanographer.

The museum, a nonprofit educational institution, was launched in the early 1930's by scholar and philanthropist Archer M. Huntington and his wife, sculptor Anna Hyatt Huntington. In 1985, a local businessman, Lloyd Noland, Jr., approached the museum about upgrading old bridle paths into a formal trail that for the first time would permit hikers to circle the lake. Noland's family had long enjoyed the museum's policy of allowing the public to use the trails. With a half million dollars of money donated by Noland, a free public trail was opened on the museum's property in October of 1991.

There are many lake-encircling paths in Virginia. The Noland Trail is in a league of its own. The forest is nicely mature, and there are oaks and pines among the overstory. Dogwood and other flowering trees add to the appeal of spring.

The trail itself is very gradual and a sandy, but dense surface permits the passage of wheelchairs and baby carriages (bicycles are prohibited). Polished stone mile markers, placed every .5 mile, are but one touch of class on this trail. Signs are beautifully routed, benches are placed often, there are designated overlooks, and fourteen wooden bridges range from small to lengthy and impressive.

The path is an easy hike, and the surface makes it wonderful for jogging.

*The Noland Trail circles Lake Maury on the grounds of The Mariner's Museum in* Newport News, *Virginia.*

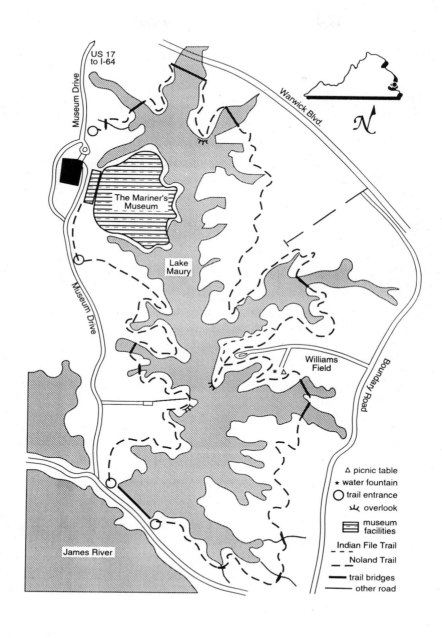

US 17
to I-64

Museum Drive

Warwick Blvd.

N

The Mariner's
Museum

Lake
Maury

Museum Drive

Williams
Field

Boundary Road

△ picnic table
★ water fountain
◯ trail entrance
〰 overlook
museum
facilities
Indian File Trail
Noland Trail
trail bridges
other road

James River

Many residents of nearby neighborhoods, especially senior citizens and families, use the new path. But the trail, like the museum, is certainly worthy of attracting visitors from throughout the region.

From the museum, trailheads lie north and south. Going north, two bridges and a viewpoint are within the first .7 mile, a nice 1.5-mile leg-stretcher for round-trip hikers. A wildflower meadow blooms at the 1.1-mile mark. Views and picnic areas are located at the Williams Field area, between two and 2.3 miles.

The first segment ends in just over three miles at the dam that separates the lake, what was once Waters Creek, from the James River. A backtrack here is a moderate 6.6-mile hike.

Crossing the dam, the trail continues another two miles to a trailhead south of the museum. Just that segment, out and back from the museum parking area, is a nice four-mile hike. The loop of the entire lake is just over five miles.

Trail use is free, but the museum asks that dogs be leashed and cleaned-up after. No alcohol is permitted, campfires are prohibited, and the lake is off limits to swimming, wading, and fishing (except from boats rented in summer from the museum).

# Seashore State Park

This nearly 3,000-acre park illustrates the difference a road makes. Easily reached by car, and located in a summer resort area, Seashore State Park is Virginia's most popular, with about one million visitors a year. Not far away, False Cape State Park boasts miles of empty beaches, but because access requires hiking or bicycling, that park is one of the state's least visited.

Luckily, Seashore offers some of the same sights, including wonderful opportunities for observing wildlife on an extensive trail system. The park's trails explore a noteworthy natural area of dunes and cypress swamps listed in the National Register of Natural Landmarks.

This is the northernmost location on the east coast where subtropical and temperate plants exist side by side. The park's interesting ecosystem spans diverse zones that include a mile-long beach, forested dunes, freshwater swamps, and scenic saltwater marshes. Spanish moss hangs on the trees in some places, giving the impression that the hiker is much farther south.

Besides raccoons, bobcats, egrets, herons, and other animals, the park is also home to ticks, many biting insects, and snakes. Carry bug repellent in the summer, and use caution to avoid snakes if you venture off trails. The copperhead and cottonmouth are indeed poisonous.

Nine trails total just over nineteen miles of hiking at Seashore State Park and have been designated as National Recreation Trails by the Department of the Interior. Six miles of those trails are also for bicycling. Though a fine place to stroll in the off-season, the public beach on the Chesapeake Bay is restricted to overnight campground guests during the summer.

The effort to create the park started in the 1920s, and by 1933, more than 2,000 acres had been assembled with the help of private citizens. The Civilian Conservation Corps undertook initial development of the park. The park now has 235 bayside campsites (camp store, bathhouses) and twenty cabins for rent by the week (available for minimum two-day stays when not rented

*Seashore State Park trails meander through the junction between the Middle Atlantic and more southerly climate zones.*

weekly). There is also a large picnic area (shelter available for rent), and a boat launch is located in the park.

Today, the popular park charges a modest parking fee ($1 per car off-season, $2-$3 per car between Memorial Day and Labor Day ). Seashore has a first-class visitor center and an outdoor education center that offers facilities and curriculum guides for school and other groups wanting serious study of the outdoors. The park's developed facilities, campground, visitor center, and picnic area are open from late March to early November.

Campground fees are charged and sites may be reserved in advance year-round for an additional fee by phone or mail from Virginia State Parks Reservation Center, P.O. Box 1895, Richmond, Virginia, 23215-1815, (800) 933-7275, 9 a.m.-4 p.m., Monday through Friday, with check, money order, Visa or MC.

The park is located just north of the public beach in Virginia Beach on US 60, about 110 miles from Richmond via Interstate 64, and US 13. **For more park information, contact: Seashore State Park, 2500 Shore Drive, VirginiaBeach, Virginia 23451, (804) 481-2131.**

# HIKE 49 *LONG CREEK TRAIL/ OSPREY TRAIL CIRCUIT*

**General description:** At just under eight miles (3.8 miles one way), this is the longest hike in the Seashore State Park that doesn't involve developed roadways. It is also the wildest, most scenic walk, and has some hilly terrain. Portions of both trails can be flooded at high tide, so be sure to factor that in to avoid disappointment and wet feet.

*Spanish moss hangs from bald cypress on the Bald Cypress Nature Trail in Seashore State Park.*

**Elevation gain and loss:** Some hilly dune areas, but minimal rise and fall in this area just above sea level.

**Water availability:** Available at the visitor center, picnic area, and campground in season. Restrooms and a water fountain are available in the off season at the visitor center.

**Finding the trailhead:** Seashore State Park is about 100 miles from Richmond, via Interstate 64. Exit Interstate 64 at US 13 and then turn right on US 60 for about 4.5 miles to the park entrance, on the right. Park at the picnic area on the right, and the trail begins about a quarter mile away on the right side of the road to the visitor center.

**The hike:** Long and scenic, the Long Creek Trail is less crowded than trails closer to the visitor center. Its eight-mile length, wild scenery, and undulating character make it the choice for experienced hikers who want to combine a workout with a backcountry experience. For even more of a workout, but less backcountry, this hike can loop back on more developed trails that increase the mileage to about nine miles.

The orange-blazed trail sets off from the roadside, crosses the first of many dunes on the trail, and reaches a bridge at the .5-mile mark. The yellow-blazed Fox Run Trail branches left at .75 mile, and near the mile mark, views open up over surrounding marshes and Broad Bay.

The Kingfisher Trail (white-blazed) leaves left at a 1.5 miles, and reaches the Cape Henry Trail in .5 mile. At 1.7 miles, the White Hill Lake Trail (gold-blazed) branches left, to the Cape Henry Trail, 1.4 miles away. This part of the trail passes through prime examples of the park's salt marsh ecosystem. Herons, egrets, and other birds and wildlife are visible in this tidal zone.

At the two mile mark, dune-top views shift from White Hill Lake, on the

146

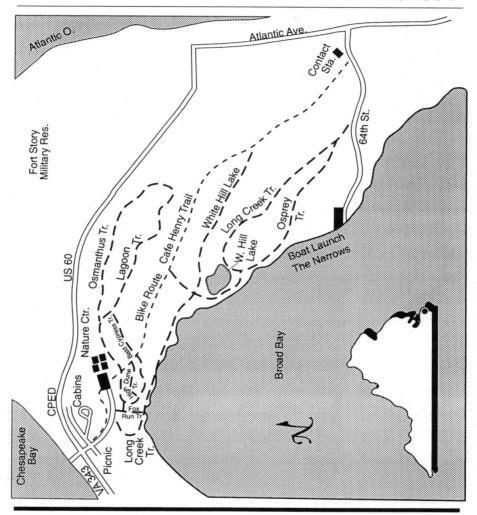

Left, to Broad Bay, on the right. Just over two miles from the start, the Long Creek Trail bears left and the green-blazed Osprey Trail goes right, both of which join farther on. The Long Creek Trail continues, with good views from the crest of an extensive dune, and reaches the junction with the Osprey Trail, on the right, at 3.3 miles.

The major road in this end of the park, 64th Street, is .5 mile away from this junction. East of the trail junction, there's a park contact station where that road leaves Atlantic Avenue.

The best trail loop is to turn right on the Osprey Trail. In .5 mile, at just under four miles, there are salt marshes and bayside views. At 4.75 miles, the Osprey Trail rejoins the Long Creek Trail just over two miles from your car. The total hike is 7.3 miles.

Hikers could expand that distance to 9.1 miles by following the Long Creek Trail to 64th Street, going left on the road .6 mile to the Cape Henry Trail, taking that 1.1 miles to the White Hill Lake Trail, and White Hill Lake Trail back to the Long Creek Trail.

# HIKE 50   *BALD CYPRESS AND OSMANTHUS TRAIL CIRCUIT*

**General description:** A fine nature trail and the longer Osmanthus Trail combine to yield an easy 1.5- to 4.6-mile introduction to this noteworthy seaside natural area. The pools and viewpoints on the Bald Cypress Trail are particularly good for observing snakes, turtles, and other forms of wildlife.
**Elevation gain and loss:** There is minimal rise and fall in this area just above sea level.
**Water availability:** Available at the visitor center, picnic area, and campground in season. Restrooms and a water fountain are available in the off-season at the trailhead.
**Finding the trailhead:** Seashore State Park is about 100 miles from Richmond, via Interstate 64. Exit Interstate 64 at US 13 and then turn right on US 60 for about 4.5 miles to the park entrance, on the right. The trail begins beside the visitor center.

**The hike:** The Bald Cypress Trail, a 1.5-mile loop, blazed red, explores the park's cypress swamp habitat on boardwalks, observation decks, and short uphill climbs over forested dunes. An interpretive booklet, available for a small fee at the visitor center, is keyed to numbered posts that offer insight into the unique ecosystem.

The Bald Cypress Trail can be shortened at a number of points, and made longer with the addition of the Osmanthus Trail. Trail options range from .3 mile to just under a mile, 1.5 miles, about four miles, and 4.5 miles.

The trail sets off on boardwalks from the visitor center and quickly has the hiker surrounded by a watery swamp where towering cypress trees are draped in Spanish moss. Boardwalks cross cypress swamps to a T-junction. To the right it's just .2 mile back to the visitor center via the Cape Henry Trail, a road-width hiking/biking trail. Go left to continue, where you'll see an observation deck to the right.

In just under .5 mile, you'll pass one, then the other junctions with the Osmanthus Trail on the left. The Bald Cypress Trail crosses forested dunes and passes swampy spots in this tangled area before reaching the Cape Henry Trail at about three-fourths of a mile. To the right, it's .2 mile to the visitor center, for a total walk of just under a mile. On the way, the High Dune Trail branches left.

Past the Cape Henry Trail, the path begins its final loop back to the visitor center. The trail is never very far from cypress swamps, and at about .9 mile, a side trail reaches an observation deck over water. The trail ascends dunes as it passes the High Dune Trail at the one mile mark. The trail crosses a few

*The Spanish moss hangs to meet cypress knees on the Bald Cypress Nature Trail in Seashore State Park.*

more dunes, then passes more trailside cypress swamps on the way back to the Cape Henry Trail and the visitor center, reached at 1.5 miles. To add a bit more exertion to the walk, include the hilly High Dunes Trail.

The blue-blazed Osmanthus Trail, named after the osmanthus tree, or wild olive, adds another 3.1 miles to the 1.5-mile Bald Cypress Trail Loop. All of that extra mileage loops through generally low, damp terrain, at times crossing bridges and boardwalks. It reenters the Bald Cypress Trail 3.1 miles from its start. Hikers who take the Bald Cypress Trail and the Osmanthus Trail loop will reach the Cape Henry Trail at about 3.75 miles. By turning right on the Cape Henry Trail to the visitor center, this loop can be just under four miles. Continuing on the Bald Cypress Trail, the total hike is about 4.5 miles back to the visitor center.

# Back Bay National Wildlife Refuge and False Cape State Park

The combination of Back Bay National Wildlife Refuge and False Cape State Park may offer the best beach hiking in the state and some of the best in the East. The park bills itself as "one of the last undisturbed coastal environments on the East Coast."

South of Virginia Beach, the Back Bay National Wildlife Refuge serves as a buffer to False Cape State Park, an isolated state preserve that backs up to the North Carolina border. False Cape is one of the least-visited Virginia state parks, but it contains one of country's best environmental education facilities for use by school, university, and special interest groups.

Not too long ago, off-road vehicles had unrestricted reign over this oceanside wilderness. Today, access is restricted to hikers, bicyclists, and canoeists. Mountain bikers and even touring cyclists can ride deep into the park, and many serious hikers and backpackers may choose to use a bike as an initial means of access.

Both the Back Bay National Wildlife Refuge, reached first from the Sandbridge area south of Virginia Beach, and then the state park are located on a "barrier spit" between the rich marshland of Back Bay and the Atlantic Ocean.

Canoeists usually paddle south along the bay side of the refuge. Crossing the bay is a tricky proposition. Back Bay is twelve miles long and five miles wide, but only four to five feet deep. That makes it a prime location for sudden squalls, high winds, and startlingly big waves. Lacking lunar tides, the bay is subject to these "wind tides." Nevertheless, two boat landings are available, and motorized access across the bay is very possible.

The 9,000-acre refuge and 4,300-acre state park offer nearly ten miles of inspiring undeveloped beaches. The refuge is a day use area only, but camping is permitted in the state park at four developed locations: two on the bay and two directly on the beach. Each camping area has three sites accommodating six campers. No open fires are permitted.

Campers must have permits ($8 per night, per site), available in person only from Seashore State Park, north of Virginia Beach, and not too far out of the way. Viewing an orientation film is a requirement, so even campers making reservations in advance (six months to a year permitted) must do so in person.

Campers must park at Little Island Park, a city of Virginia Beach facility at the entrance to the wildlife refuge. Overnight parking at the park and all parking in the refuge requires a parking fee. Per car parking rates in season (Memorial Day weekend to Labor Day) at Little Island are $4 on weekdays, $5 on weekends, and $10 for buses. No charge at other times of year. Refuge parking fees are $4 per car and $1 for bicycles, daytime only.

From Little Island, there is a 1.3-mile walk or ride on asphalt before reaching the day use parking area and the start of more rustic trails.

Different seasons create different hiking experiences, so the best time for you to visit depends on what experience you want. Summer is hot and humid, and with no water available in the park, hikers and campers must carry large quantities of water (one gallon a day is recommended). Also carry a tarp for campsite shade, plenty of sunscreen, a large hat, and a lot of insect repellent. The combination of beach and marsh makes for a very buggy environment. Snakes include the poisonous cottonmouth moccasin. Breezy, and therefore almost bugless, beach campsites are best in summer.

October (closed one week in October for hunting) to March may be the best time to go. Bugs and snakes vanish, the humidity drops, the air clears, and migrating waterfowl are profuse. A diversity of campsites and a well-developed trail system permit visitors to sample the diverse ecosystems that attract that waterfowl.

The beaches feed into a barrier of dunes, some of them quite high. The largest of these dunes were actually constructed by the Civilian Conservation Corps in the early 1930s. The dunes are barriers to salt spray and wind, so a shrubby, grass-covered area of stable vegetation forms on their protected side. That shelters the maritime forest zone, an area of loblolly pine and live oak. In fact, this area is one of the northernmost growing locations of live oak. Deer, raccoons, rabbits, and wild pigs and horses inhabit this ecosystem.

Behind the maritime forest, conditions are sufficiently stable for a a layer of soil to form on the sand. An oak/pine forest grows here and fuses with the marshy edge of the bay, actually a very isolated sound between the barrier spit and the mainland.

Settlement of the False Cape State Park area was sparse. Mariners falsely identified the subtle bulge as Cape Henry, which is farther north, and were lured to their demise in the "false cape." Early settlers were seamen from those doomed ships, as well as Coast Guardsmen staffing early life-saving stations. In one instance, a load of shipwrecked lumber was used to build a church.

Today the park's Wash Woods Environmental Education Center (EEC) is located near that church and other homes that still stand . The facility is housed in the clubhouse of one of the many hunt clubs that used the area from the turn of the century to the 1960s when the park was created. The EEC is an overnight facility ($200 each night) that includes sleeping for twenty-two, kitchen facilities, and the use of wet lab/aquarium.

The center has its own pontoon boat for educational bay tours ($75/fifteen people) offered on three different topics by a park pilot/interpreter. To be able to use the center, the park must receive a lesson plan showing how the center will fit into the program of study.

Use of the EEC is one of the best ways to see the park. EEC groups are bussed in to the facility ($36 round trip, per group), but however you get there, Back Bay and False Cape offer a nationally significant trail experience.

The two parks are located twenty miles south of the boardwalk in Virginia Beach. From Interstate 64, take Indian River Road east to Newbridge Road. Take Newbridge to Sandbridge, then go south on Sandpiper Road four miles to the Little Island Park and the Back Bay National Wildlife Refuge.

**For further information, including reasonable trail maps, contact: Back Bay National Wildlife Refuge, 4005 Sandpiper Road, Virginia Beach, Virginia 23456, 804-721-2412; or False Cape State Park, 4001 Sandpiper Road, Virginia Beach, Virginia 23456, 804-426-7128.**

# HIKE 51 *BACK BAY/FALSE CAPE TRAILS*

**General description:** Sixteen trails in the Back Bay National Wildlife Refuge and False Cape State Park that offer day and overnight beach and marsh hikes between Sandbridge, Virginia, and the North Carolina state line.

**Elevation gain and loss:** Maximum elevation on dunes is about twenty-five feet.

**Water availability:** Restrooms are available in season (Memorial weekend to Labor Day) at Little Island Park, but there is no formal water source, and no drinking water is available along the trails.

**Finding the trailhead:** See description under introduction to Back Bay Wildlife Refuge and False Cape State Park.

**The hike:** From the Little Island parking area at the refuge boundary, over-

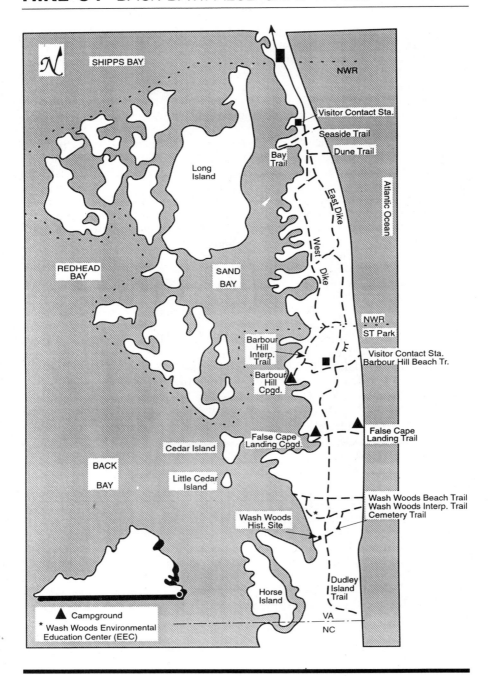

SHIPPS BAY

NWR

Visitor Contact Sta.

Seaside Trail

Dune Trail

Bay Trail

Long Island

East Dike

Atlantic Ocean

West Dike

REDHEAD BAY

SAND BAY

NWR

ST Park

Visitor Contact Sta.
Barbour Hill Beach Tr.

Barbour Hill Interp. Trail

Barbour Hill Cpgd.

False Cape Landing Trail

False Cape Landing Cpgd.

Cedar Island

BACK BAY

Little Cedar Island

Wash Woods Beach Trail
Wash Woods Interp. Trail
Cemetery Trail

Wash Woods Hist. Site

Dudley Island Trail

Horse Island

VA

NC

▲ Campground
* Wash Woods Environmental
  Education Center (EEC)

night hikers and bikers head south on the paved road to the refuge contact station and parking area for day users. At this point, 1.3 miles from Little Island Park, the real hiking begins, so mileages are measured from here. (Overnighters should add 1.3 miles to those figures.)

Hikers heading to False Cape State Park will choose either the east or west dike routes, so named because they are trails second and water impoundment dikes first. They are gravel-topped and well-suited for cycling, and they follow the bay or dune side of the barrier spit that separates the Atlantic from Back Bay.

Near the refuge parking area, the dike trails start off together, and three side trails branch affording short strolls. The Bay Trail heads west .5 mile to Back Bay. The Seaside Trail follows a boardwalk east to the beach in a quarter mile. The furthest south of the three side trails is the Dune Trail, another boardwalk that heads east to the beach in .5 mile. The east and west dikes split just before the Dune Trail, so take the east dike to reach the Dune Trail.

Whichever trail you take south, cross dike routes connect the two at two miles, 2.5 miles, and again at the state park line. The dikes create three impoundments that are drained in summer and then filled and planted with grasses and other plants that serve as winter feed and habitat for wintering wildfowl, including snow geese, Canada geese, tundra swans, and many others.

Trail users enter the state park at 3.5 miles and are immediately on the Barbour Hill Interpretive Trail, a 2.4 mile nature loop with viewpoints and numbered posts keyed to a brochure. A branch of this hiker/biker trail leads west to a camping area. The trail reaches the state park contact station in another .75 mile, about 4.25 miles from the refuge visitor contact station. From the state park contact station, the Barbour Hill Beach Trail ascends over the dunes to another campground, and the Atlantic Ocean, in .7 mile.

The main trail continues another 2.3 miles (6.5 from the refuge contact station) before reaching bay and beach campgrounds at False Cape Landing. The False Cape Landing Trail reaches the beach and campsites .6 mile from the main trail.

Another 1.2 mile walk on the main trail (7.7 miles from refuge contact station) reaches a cluster of trails at the Wash Woods Environmental Education Center. Three quarters of a mile separates two trails that reach the beach—the Wash Woods Beach Trail, which reaches the Atlantic in .8 mile, and the Wash Woods Interpretive Trail, which reaches the ocean in .7 mile. The .5-mile cemetery trail dips south from the Wash Woods Interpretive Trail, crosses the main trail, and reaches a cemetery and church site that recall the small community that once existed in this remote area.

This is the southernmost location of developed facilities in the park, and bicycles are not permitted beyond this point. The Dudley Island Trail leads hikers another three miles south past the Wash Woods Environmental Education Center into the park's most primitive areas. The trail ends at a pristine beach at the North Carolina state line, about ten miles from the refuge visitor contact station.

Together, these two parks can afford a lengthy, memorable trip to one of the last places on the Atlantic coast that remains largely unaffected by man. Backpackers can enjoy beach camping amid total solitude. For the dedicated mountain biker, an easy ride and a short hike lead to sunbathing on virtually private beaches.

Though the Wash Woods Environmental Education Center is a long way from the parking area, the park offers motorized transportation. This is surely one of the best such facilities in the country. Less ambitious groups can also enjoy

*The southernmost trails in False Cape State Park offer true seaside solitude.*

nature study at the Barbour Hill Interpretive Trail. Though four miles from the parking area, easy bicycling paths make the area accessible to schools, scout troops, and other groups.

## Chincoteague National Wildlife Refuge and Trails

# HIKE 52 — *THE WILDLIFE LOOP, THE SERVICE ROAD, THE LIGHTHOUSE TRAIL, THE WOODLAND TRAIL*

**General description:** This spectacular Barrier Island wildlife area on Virginia's Eastern Shore, part of the Assateague Island National Seashore, is famous for its herd of free-roaming ponies. A variety of trails include a .25-mile path to a lighthouse, miles of beach backpacking, and a 1.6-mile woodland walk to possible views of the island's ponies.

**Elevation gain and loss:** Negligible.

**Trailhead elevations:** Between six and ten feet above sea level.

**High point:** Approximately twenty-two feet at the base of the lighthouse.

**Water availability:** Water is available in season at the developed facilities in the refuge, including the Chincoteague Refuge Visitor Center, which is run by the U.S. Fish & Wildlife Service, and the Toms Cove Visitor Center, operated by the National Park Service. In winter, the Refuge Visitor Center is the choice for water, available in the year-round restrooms. The Toms Cove

*The trails of Chincoteague National Wildlife Refuge offer encounters with the island's famous ponies.* Photo courtesy of Chincoteague National Wildlife Refuge.

Visitor Center is open in the winter, but restrooms and beachside bathhouses are closed. Non-flush restrooms are available. Bringing water from the village of Chincoteague, the last stop before the refuge, may be most convenient. **Finding the trailhead:** Chincoteague National Wildlife Refuge is located on Virginia's Eastern Shore, Assateague Island, at the Maryland border. Access from northern Virginia is best over the Chesapeake Bay Bridge east of Annapolis. From elsewhere, the choice route is over the Chesapeake Bay Bridge-Tunnel, a seventeen-mile over and underwater route listed as one of the seven wonders of the modern world by the American Society of Engineers.

The refuge is approximately seventy-five miles north of the Bridge-Tunnel adjacent to the village of Chincoteague. The refuge can be a bit confusing to find. After crossing the bridge into Chincoteague on VA 175, turn left on Main Street and proceed a short distance to Maddox Boulevard (State Route 2113). Turn right onto Maddox at a green "Assateague" sign strung across Main Street above street level signs. The refuge is then straight ahead, about two miles. **For more information:** Chincoteague National Wildlife Refuge, P.O. Box 62, Chincoteague, VA 23336, (804) 336-6122. Also contact: Assateague Island National Seashore, Route 611, 7206 National Seashore Lane, Berlin, MD 21811, (410) 641-3030, or (410) 641-1441.

**The hike:** The Virginia portion of thirty-seven-mile-long Assateague Island is the approximately 10,000-acre Chincoteague National Wildlife Refuge. The island also contains substantial national park land and a Maryland state park. All of these preserves are known as the Assateague National Seashore and collectively managed by the National Park Service, U.S. Fish & Wildlife Service, and the Maryland Department of Natural Resources.

Early in this century, with more and more coastal land being developed,

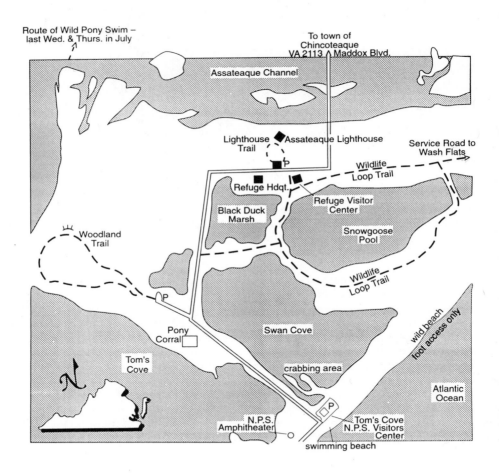

Route of Wild Pony Swim – last Wed. & Thurs. in July

To town of Chincoteaque
VA 2113 / Maddox Blvd.

Assateaque Channel

Lighthouse Trail

Assateaque Lighthouse

Service Road to Wash Flats

Wildlife Loop Trail

Refuge Hdqt.

Refuge Visitor Center

Black Duck Marsh

Woodland Trail

Snowgoose Pool

Wildlife Loop Trail

Pony Corral

Swan Cove

Tom's Cove

wild beach foot access only

crabbing area

Atlantic Ocean

N.P.S. Amphitheater

Tom's Cove N.P.S. Visitors Center

swimming beach

*On Virginia's easier trails, hiking is a family activity.*

and birds being hunted for sport and plumage, a dramatic decline in water-fowl populations was taking place. The refuge was established in 1943 to help halt that trend.

Today the refuge actively protects many species of migratory waterfowl and their habitat. In this case, actively means manipulating wetlands to provide the habitat necessary at different times of year. To that end, the refuge includes manmade water impoundments.

Some of Assateague Island's best opportunities to observe waterfowl occur at the water impoundments found off the Chincoteague National Wildlife Refuge. Many of the trails described here offer access to those areas. But remember, national wildlife refuges are different from parks managed for recreation. If a specific area isn't designated as open for recreation, it is considered closed. In fact, normally open parts of the refuge may be closed when birds are nesting. Obey all signs restricting use. That emphasis on wildlife is the reason why all pets are prohibited in the refuge and national seashore.

During the summer, hikers will find a variety of interpretive programs available at the refuge. Much of that focuses on wildlife. Mammals seen in the refuge include rabbits, sika deer (an introduced Oriental species), muskrats, opossums, and fox squirrels.

Loggerhead turtles are present, but not poisonous snakes. Birds often seen at the refuge include a variety of ducks, egrets, herons, loons, mergansers, and even very rare, protected birds such as the piping plover. For birdwatchers, Chincoteague is a real destination.

A variety of hikes are described below, but none are suitable for backpacking. Backpackers should focus on the ten-mile beachfront part of the refuge, accessible from the Toms Cove Visitor Center where camping permits are available. Backpackers could make the thirty-five-mile trek to

Maryland's seashore facilities and be picked up there, or just trek out and back.

If an out-and-back backpacking trip is your goal, remember that you must carry substantial water, and use designated campsites. The first is just inside Maryland, so overnighters will need to hike eleven miles before camping. If you visit in summer, bring insect repellent and sunscreen. Ticks and mosquitoes can be a problem during the warm months, so plan accordingly.

## The Wildlife Loop

This 3.2-mile paved loop trail is actually a road. It is reserved for hikers and bicyclists during the day until three p.m. After that, motorists are permitted on the route, a nice circle around Snow Goose Pool.

The hike begins at the Chincoteague Refuge Visitor Center, the first left once inside the refuge. Travelling counterclockwise, the first portion of the route is wooded on the left and passes fresh water impoundments on the right, used to enhance nesting and feeding areas for wildlife. On the right, just past Black Duck Marsh, a side trail goes right Beach Road.

The more distant part of the loop is wood. As hikers return toward the visitor, center, they cross Snow Goose Pool on a dike and then go left back to the visitor center. To the right, the Service Road goes to Wash Flats; see that trail entry. The Wildlife Loop has two observation decks.

## The Service Road

Hiking clockwise on the Wildlife Loop, against the normal flow of traffic, hikers can go straight at the first turn on the Wildlife Loop and walk an approximately seven-mile service road deep into the Wash Flats area of the refuge, a 1000-acre impoundment that offers excellent opportunities to view wildlife. An up to fourteen-mile round-trip is possible. The earthen surfaced, road-width trail is actually a dike created when the impoundments were excavated.

Hikers should use caution to stay on the trail. Even though hikers could leave the trail in several areas, rangers stress that that is not permitted. This area is primarily a home to wildlife, not a recreation area.

## The Lighthouse Trail

On this short, easy .25-mile loop, hikers climb to the locally lofty elevation of twenty-two feet. That is the elevation at the base of the Assateague Lighthouse, an active U.S. Coast Guard facility that is closed to the public. The 142-foot high striped lighthouse was built in 1833 for $55,000. The trail starts just east of the refuge headquarters.

## The Woodland Trail

Another paved route, the Woodland Trail is a 1.6-mile hiking/biking loop path. Hikers follow the trail through a dense loblolly pine forest to the edge of a marsh, a spot preferred by the wild ponies that live on the island. Hikers often see the ponies from an observation deck on the trail, located about a third of the way around the loop when hiking counterclockwise.

The Woodland Trail is reached from Beach Road on the way to the Toms Cove Visitor Center.

# ABOUT THE AUTHOR

Travel and outdoor writer, and photographer, Randy Johnson, is a member of the Society of American Travel Writers and the North American Ski Journalist's Association. He specializes in the South, and its mountains. Johnson resides in Boone, North Carolina where he is a contributing editor for the *Mountain Times,* in Boone, and Senior Editor at *Hemispheres,* United Airlines travel magazine, based in Greensboro. Among his magazine credits are *Ski, Cross Country Skier, American Forests, Snow Country, Canoe, Backpacker,* and others. His newspaper articles and photos appear in *The Atlanta Journal-Constitution, Charlotte Observer, Boston Globe, Richmond Time-Dispatch,* and *Raleigh News and Observer.*

# FALCON GUIDES    *Perfect for every outdoor adventure!*

Angler's Guide to Alaska
Angler's Guide to Florida
Angler's Guide to Montana
Backcountry Horseman's Guide to Washington
Birder's Guide to Montana
Birding Arizona
Birding Minnesota
Floater's Guide to Colorado
Floater's Guide to Missouri
Floater's Guide to Montana
Hiker's Guide to Alaska
Hiking Alberta
Hiker's Guide to Arizona
Hiking Arizona's Cactus Country
Hiking the Beartooths
Hiking Big Bend National Park
Hiking California
Hiking Carlsbad Caverns and Guadalupe National Park
Hiking Colorado
Hiker's Guide to Florida
Hiker's Guide to Georgia
Hiking Glacier/Waterton Lakes National Parks
Hiking Hot Springs in the Pacific Northwest
Hiker's Guide to Idaho
Hiking Maine
Hiking Michigan
Hiking Montana
Hiker's Guide to Montana's Continental Divide Trail
Hiker's Guide to Nevada
Hiking New Hampshire
Hiking New Mexico
Hiking North Carolina
Hiker's Guide to Oregon
Hiking Oregon's Eagle Cap Wilderness
Hiking Tennessee
Hiking Texas
Hiker's Guide to Utah
Hiking Virginia
Hiker's Guide to Washington
Hiker's Guide to Wyoming
Trail Guide to Bob Marshall Country
Trail Guide to Olympic National Park
Wild Montana
Rockhounding Arizona
Rockhound's Guide to California
Rockhound's Guide to Colorado
Rockhound's Guide to Montana
Rockhound's Guide to New Mexico
Rockhound's Guide to Texas

Rock Climbing Colorado
Rock Climber's Guide to Montana
Scenic Byways
Scenic Byways II
Back Country Byways
Scenic Driving Arizona
Scenic Driving California
Scenic Driving Colorado
Scenic Driving Georgia
Scenic Driving Montana
Scenic Driving New Mexico
Oregon Scenic Drives
Scenic Driving Texas
Traveler's Guide to the Lewis & Clark Trail
Traveler's Guide to the Oregon Trail
Traveler's Guide to the Pony Express Trail
Mountain Biking Arizona
Mountain Biker's Guide to Central Appalachia
Mountain Biker's Guide to Colorado
Mountain Biking the Great Lake States
Mountain Biking the Great Plains States
Mountain Biking the Midwest
Mountain Biker's Guide to the Ozarks
Mountain Biker's Guide to New Mexico
Mountain Biker's Guide to Northern California/Nevada
Mountain Biking Northern New England
Mountain Biker's Guide to the Northern Rockies
Mountain Biking the Pacific Northwest
Mountain Biking the Southeast
Mountain Biker's Guide to Southern California
Mountain Biker's Guide to Southern New England
Mountain Biker's Guide to the Southwest
Mountain Biking Texas and Oklahoma
Mountain Biker's Guide to Utah
Wild Country Companion

# FALCON
## 1-800-582-2665

P.O. BOX 1718
HELENA, MT  59624